To Denise & Anthony

With warm blessings on
you both,
In Christ,

Dan & Katie Montgomery

B-DAY
11/08/96

Beauty in the Stone

How God Sculpts You into the Image of Christ

Dr. Dan Montgomery

THOMAS NELSON PUBLISHERS
Nashville • Atlanta • London • Vancouver

Published in Nashville, Tennessee, by Thomas Nelson, Inc., Publishers, and distributed in Canada by Word Communications, Ltd., Richmond, British Columbia.

Unless otherwise noted, Scripture quotations in this publication are from THE NEW KING JAMES VERSION. Copyright © 1979, 1980, 1982, Thomas Nelson, Inc., Publishers. Scripture quotations marked KJV are from The King James Version of the Holy Bible. Scripture quotations marked TLB are taken from *The Living Bible,* copyright 1971 by Tyndale House Publishers, Wheaton, Illinois. Used by permission. Scripture quotations marked MESSAGE are from *The Message: The New Testament in Contemporary English.* Copyright 1993 by Eugene H. Peterson. Scripture quotations noted NRSV are from the New Revised Standard Version of the Bible. Copyright © 1989 by the Division of Christian Education of the National Council of the Churches of Christ in the United States of America.

Some material in Chapters 5, 14, and 17 originally appeared in *Guideposts.*

Library of Congress Cataloging-in-Publication Data

Montgomery, Dan, 1946–
    Beauty in the stone : how God sculpts you into the image of Christ / Dan Montgomery.
        p.   cm.
    Includes bibliographical references.
    ISBN 0-7852-7745-5 (hardcover)
    1. Personality—Religious aspects—Christianity.   2. Typology (Psychology)—Religious aspects—Christianity.   3. Counseling—Religious aspects—Christianity.   4. Christian life.   5. Jesus Christ—Psychology.   I. Title.
BV4597.57.M66   1996
233'.5—dc20   95-51452
                                                                                                        CIP

Printed in the United States of America.

1 2 3 4 5 6 — 01 00 99 98 97 96

To my darlin' Kate.

*My heart is brimming over as I
dedicate this book to Katie Montgomery
—my wife, editor, and helpmate.*

About the Author

Dr. Dan Montgomery is a licensed clinical psychologist with advanced degrees in psychology and philosophy and twenty-five thousand hours of counseling experience. In addition to his work in private practice, he has taught in four universities. An internationally known conference speaker, his magazine articles have been read by thirty million people worldwide. Dr. Montgomery may be contacted at the address and phone number below:

681 Portofino Lane
Foster City, CA 94404

(415) 345-8018

Contents

CONTENTS

Foreword

Do you ever wonder, Whatever is this going on inside me? Why am I afraid? Worried? Angry? What's bugging me?

If you knew Dan Montgomery like I know Dan Montgomery, you'd do what I do. You'd give him a ring. "Hey, Dan, take me down inside myself. Help me corner this demon." And he would. How do I know? Because Dan is my favorite sorter-outer of my inner goings-on.

He'll be yours, too, when you've read *Beauty in the Stone*. Why? Because he'll assure you, you're nowhere near as crazy as you thought you were. All those get-even wishes and evil thoughts aren't the real you. Neither is the phoney "Big Shot" you trot out now and then. Or his opposite, "The Cowering Timid Soul" you've faked sometimes.

"Perfectionist," "Con Artist," "Prima Donna": All of these wooly buggers come parading before us in this book. Probing. Embarrassing. Revealing. Healing. A book that says, "Laugh. Cry. Think. Change." And when you're through you will say, "Thank you, Dan. From now on you're one of my favorite authors too. I can see what Charlie means. Next time I need you I'll give you a ring."

Charlie Shedd
Author of the Multimillion-Sellers
Letters to Karen and *Letters to Philip*

Introduction

I'm wondering what has brought you to read this book. Are you seeking to heal your personality and relationships? Are you searching for a deeper closeness to God and a greater grasp of your calling? Or are you skeptical that connecting God with psychology can be of any use?

I can identify with all three of these questions. I've passionately sought from God the healing of my personality and relationships. I've yearned for a closer relationship with Him and some grasp of my mission in life. And, yes, I've had times in life when I wondered whether God and psychology had anything to do with each other.

I knew I needed healing, even as a teenager. Beaten up and chased by gang members, I built an aggressive persona to survive. I rarely smiled. I beat up people. My fierce pride blocked me from seeking help.

To make the darkness inside me more tolerable, I resigned myself to a bitter cynicism that even God couldn't help a person like me. But God didn't give up on me. He pursued me in my youth like the hound of heaven in Francis Thompson's famous poem until at last I put down my stubborn pride and melted in the presence of His healing love. At age seventeen, I said a humble prayer in an old-fashioned church service. That night, the Lord Jesus Christ entered my heart. So began the gradual transformation of my personality—confused though I was—through the mysterious ways of God.

Later in life, God called me to become a psychologist. I was studying for the ministry at the time and only reluctantly left seminary to follow that calling. During my doctoral studies in counseling, the faculty practically forced me into facing my personality flaws and rigidities. God was inviting me to look at myself in ways I'd never dreamed were necessary.

What more does God want from me than my faith in Him? I wondered. Slowly, I discovered that God wanted me to admit my secret fears, frustrations, arrogance, guilt, self-absorption, dependencies, and depression. Only then could He guide me to health and happiness.

Could it be that in God's psychology, we must face our personality flaws and confess our inability to change without His love? I believe that the God of Abraham, Isaac, and Jacob so cherishes our personalities that He wants to bring out the best of us in spite of all our resistances. In so doing, He makes us capable of real love.

This book is not just about our flawed personalities and nature; it shows practical ways to grow more whole wherever we're at. Many positive qualities lying dormant within us are awakened when we understand and surrender to the wisdom of God's psychology.

I share a lot of my pain and joy in this book, so don't feel alone as you read it. I'm right here with you, confessing my inadequacies and celebrating our mutual progress toward health and happiness by the grace of God!

PART 1

The Self
Compass

To live a spiritual life means first of all to come to the awareness of the inner polarities between which we are held in tension.

—Henri Nouwen
  *Reaching Out: The Three Movements
  of the Spiritual Life*

CHAPTER 1

Are There Laws of Personality?

Be holy, for I am holy.
—1 Peter 1:16

Are you too loving? Giving? Volunteering? Always feeling for others, but neglecting yourself?

Or are you angry much of the time? Irritable? Argumentative? Needing to get your way or get even?

What about others—people with whom you live and work? You probably know people who seem weak and helpless. No matter how much you try to support them, they remain forlorn. Or what about those who are too strong and overbearing? You get the sense that they feel superior to you and always need to control you.

What is the key to understanding these patterns? Is there a compass of personality that can give us our bearings when it comes to ourselves and other people? Is there such a thing as God's psychology?

I believe that Jesus has an answer. In fact, Jesus *is* the answer. The names of Christ reveal important aspects of His personality. Four names in particular show how He followed His inner compass—the self compass. Just as a physical compass has four points to guide in the right direction, so the self compass has four points—*love, assertion, weakness,* and *strength*—that epitomize Christ's wholeness.

The Rose of Sharon captures Christ's *love* compass point. His love is incredibly pure. He forgives our faults and reaches out with a helping hand. "I have come that they may have life," He said, "and that they may have it more abundantly" (John 10:10). Jesus is the Lover of the human soul, the original and everlasting Good Samaritan.

Remember the woman who was about to be stoned to death for adultery? She looked through a veil of tears and saw Jesus. His compassion bathed her emotional wounds. He forgave her sins and offered her a new life. She left the stoning place unharmed, God's love infusing her being.

Christ wasn't loving in every situation, however, or He would have bent over backward to please everyone. His love compass point was offset by His *assertion,* or righteous indignation. The Lion of Judah is the name that expresses Christ's assertion compass point. A fierce opponent of injustice, Christ stood up for the poor and the meek.

Jesus drove the money changers out of His Father's temple. He rebuked evildoers and challenged self-righteous Pharisees: "But woe to you Pharisees! For you tithe mint and rue and all manner of herbs, and pass by justice and the love of God" (Luke 11:42). Jesus even confronted the devil: "Away with you, Satan! For it is written, 'You shall worship the LORD your God, and Him only you shall serve'" (Matt. 4:10).

Love and assertion by themselves fall short of describing Christ's complete personality. The Lamb of God—the symbol of His redemptive mission—shows His vulnerability. How did the Son of

God experience the *weakness* compass point? Jesus shuddered with fear and dread in the Garden of Gethsemane, foreseeing the horror of the Cross. During His crucifixion, He yelled out, "My God, My God, why have You forsaken Me?" (Mark 15:34). Through weakness He became a living sacrifice for our sins. "For though He was crucified in weakness, yet He lives by the power of God" (2 Cor. 13:4).

Jesus died in His weakness only to be raised from the dead as the Prince of Peace—His *strength* compass point. The Father placed Him in authority over all creation:

> And the government will be upon His shoulder.
> And His name will be called Wonderful, Counselor, Mighty God,
> Everlasting Father, Prince of Peace (Isa. 9:6).

Because of Christ's wholeness, His eternal power is the strength of a loving servant, not the militant rule of a despot. His strength is tempered by love, assertion, and weakness.

Jesus—the Son of God and the Son of man—is a marvelously whole person. He calls us to use God's psychology to find a similar wholeness in ourselves.

THE LAWS OF PERSONALITY

Hear the health in what Jesus says to us:

> Are you tired? Worn out? Burned out on religion? Come to me. Get away with me and you'll recover your life. I'll show you how to take a real rest. Walk with me and work with me—watch how I do it. Learn the unforced rhythms of grace. I won't lay anything heavy or ill-fitting on you. Keep company with me and you'll learn to live freely and lightly (Matt. 11:28–30 MESSAGE).

Jesus draws out our potential for love, assertion, weakness, and strength. If we let Him, Jesus helps us find our way to health and happiness.

As a Christian psychologist, I feel passionately about helping people become aware of Christ in their quest for wholeness. How do we find a rhythm of grace between *Love, Assertion, Weakness,* and *Strength?* By taking the first letter of each compass point, we can refer to these as the LAWS of God's psychology. Together, they form the self compass (see fig. 1.1).

Exercising four compass points instead of just one or two allows us to be more of our real selves. The image of God can shine through us. Each of us becomes an original in Christ.

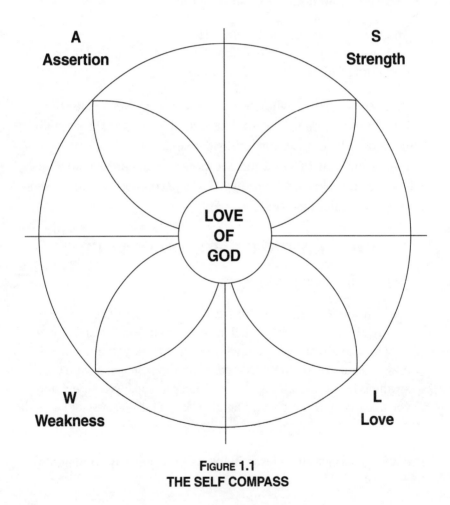

FIGURE 1.1
THE SELF COMPASS

But what happens when we unknowingly break these LAWS? What are the consequences of neglecting to read our self compass?

Original sin, or the fall of humanity from the image and purposes of God, affects every human being. Whether the negative effects of sin are transmitted to us through genes and chromosomes, early childhood experiences, or psychosocial environment, the result is that our lives fall short of what God intends.

Jesus Christ came to remedy the situation—to forgive our sins and give us bearings for health and happiness: "Do not be conformed to this world, but be transformed by the renewing of your mind, that you may prove what is that good and acceptable and perfect will of God" (Rom. 12:2).

If we accept Him as Savior and then yield our personalities to His influence, He helps us participate in God's personality. "But we all . . . beholding as in a mirror the glory of the Lord, are being transformed into the same image from glory to glory, just as by the Spirit of the Lord" (2 Cor. 3:18). However, many Christians do not understand how to use the self compass that God's psychology provides. They may not realize that their self compass is out of whack.

What about you? Are there troubles perplexing you? So often we believe that other people are causing our difficulties when the real barriers are within ourselves.

TOO MUCH LOVE

Cindy was raised a pastor's daughter. Her mom chided her about what people might think. She pleased people at all costs. She avoided conflict by never expressing an opinion. She said yes to every request of her time and energy. She typed papers for other students, sang at weddings, and played the piano at funerals.

Cindy married a pastor. After ten years of ministry she felt exhausted. In a first counseling session, Cindy blushed and stammered, "I feel selfish asking for help. I'm supposed to always think of others. People would be disappointed in me if they knew how empty I feel."

"Have you always kept your feelings a secret?" I asked.

"Of course," she said, nodding and biting her lip. "I'd never tell anyone how I really feel! I put on my smile and try to make others happy."

"What do you suppose is behind your emptiness?" I asked.

She fidgeted in her seat. "I don't know who I am. I've always lived up to other people's expectations. I don't have a single friend I can confide in!"

"Maybe it's time for you to give up your need for everyone's approval and develop some strength and assertion."

Tears welling in her eyes, Cindy agreed that it was time.

TOO MUCH ASSERTION

Jesus was assertive without becoming hateful, argumentative, or cruel. He forgave us all from the cross. But some Christians, unlike the Lord, are aggressive and unforgiving.

Frank is a successful engineer and deacon in his church. When I first met him, he seemed charming and friendly. Yet the more he talked, the more I discerned a pattern of chronic anger toward others.

"I do my best and work hard all the time," he said, sitting forward in his chair. "But my wife doesn't appreciate all my effort. She says I don't pay attention to her, and that makes me mad. My three-year-old daughter doesn't do what I tell her, and that ticks me off. My staff at work think I'm too impatient."

At our next session I showed Frank the results of his personality assessment—a test that reveals personality traits. All his life he'd blamed and attacked others, believing that they were the reason for his discontent. But the assessment revealed that Frank's aggressive personality was the problem. He was stuck on the assertion compass point.

"The behavior of this man," the assessment read, "is typified by sullen and irritable temperament, an edgy impatience, the potential for assaultiveness, and a chronic bitterness and resentment."

Frank had slapped his wife once. He often yelled at his little girl. To operate successfully as a husband and father, he needed to activate the love, weakness, and strength of his self compass.

TOO MUCH WEAKNESS

Mary came to see me regarding her unshakable sense of inner shame. She lived alone. She was a wallflower in social situations and had no close friends. She worked in a pet store cleaning fish tanks. "God loves other people. But He's ashamed of me. I think He wants to punish me for being such a bad person," she said, her voice trembling. "I was sexually molested by my brother at the age of twelve. God wants me to live alone because I'm damaged goods."

Mary was equally tormented by her fears of rejection by others. "No one wants to be around me. I'm such a klutz, and I never know what to say." Gazing down, she said, "I think people make fun of me." Mary's pattern of feeling rejected by God and ridiculed by people revealed that she was stuck on the weakness compass point. She needed help to develop love, strength, and assertion— her true potential in Christ.

TOO MUCH STRENGTH

Gary came to counseling unwillingly. He had been put on probation at work where he was a systems analyst.

"People think I'm too overbearing," he said, lifting his chin. "I know exactly what I'm doing in my job. Why won't people listen to me? No one else really understands my area as well as I do. I just like to get in there and get the job done. Everybody else wastes time. They moan and complain instead of doing what I tell them."

"So you think you're smarter than everybody else," I said.

"Well, yes, I am," said Gary with a smile. "When I'm conducting a committee meeting, I'm the only one who comes up with ideas that work. Nobody else follows through on details like I do. I don't understand what their problem is with me. I'm there earlier than anybody else, and the parking lot is empty when I leave. What more could they want?"

I got Gary's permission to talk to his boss. I wanted someone else's feedback about Gary's behavior.

"Gary is really competent in his field," his boss said. "But he's also impatient with everyone. He gets arrogant and bossy and offends people without knowing it. He's a brain without a heart."

Gary was stuck on the strength compass point and needed to discover love and weakness.

MANY MISERIES ARE OPTIONAL

When we recognize where we are stuck on the self compass, we can grow and change. By admitting our shortcomings, we can surrender more of our whole selves to Christ.

In Christ, the final work of salvation saves us from death and hell. But the ongoing work of redemption gradually transforms our imperfect personalities until in heaven we are whole like Jesus. A rigid personality keeps God at arm's length. We forestall the healing and wholeness that we are called to embrace.

God's psychology helps Christians to become competent and *strong,* yet humbly aware of *weakness* and need. They can express tender *love* to nourish others or use diplomatic *assertion* to stand against unfairness. Healthy people maintain free and equal access to all four poles of the inner personality compass, rightly using God's psychology.

Together, these compass points help us in the process of becoming whole:

- *L*ove is the glue in relationships that provides interest, caring, and tenderness. Through love, we approach God heart to heart.

- *A*ssertion enables us to stand up for ourselves and brings a sense of courage, self-preservation, and righteous indignation. Through assertion, we approach God with boldness.

- *W*eakness expresses our limitations and dependence on God—offering humility, surrender, and patience. Through weakness, we approach God in need.

- *S*trength reflects our self-worth and fosters personal confidence, poise, and identity. Through strength, we approach God in praise.

You may ask, "If we all use the same compass, won't we become boring look-alikes?" Was Jesus boring because of His wholeness? Hardly. He was utterly unpredictable. Christ would stop teaching in order to take little children in His arms and bless them. He'd confront stolid religious leaders only to bare His heart to His disciples a few minutes later. He warmed the hearts of the two men on the road to Emmaus but disappeared as soon as they recognized Him.

No matter who we are, love and assertion and weakness and strength let us radiate our uniqueness—to be free and creative in fulfilling our destinies. Our communication with others is heartfelt. We enjoy the benefits of God's psychology.

When our self compass is skewed, it makes us boring, predictable, and insincere. People who resist wholeness are rigid in thinking, feeling, and relating. Communication with others tends to be stilted and unimaginative.

> *When our self compass is skewed, it makes us boring, predictable, and insincere.*

Unknowingly, they can thwart the wisdom of God's psychology for creative living.

WE NEED REGULAR COMPASS ALIGNMENT

How does a skewed self compass affect us? Nine months ago I noticed a shimmy in the steering wheel of my Thunderbird. I ignored it, hoping it might go away. It got worse. Last week, I finally took it to a mechanic. He aligned the wheels. The shimmy disappeared.

I paid a price for not facing this symptom sooner. I had to replace all four tires—30,000 miles before they normally would have worn out. Moral: unless we use all four points of the self compass, there will be considerable wear and tear on us, our families, and God's mission for us.

Everyone's inner self needs continuous alignment so that life runs more smoothly. The Holy Spirit is the mechanic of our souls, ably diagnosing our needs and assisting us toward wholeness. But just as I had to make my car available for repairs, so we must face our imperfections and humbly submit them to God.

If we invite the Holy Spirit's help, He becomes an ever-present force for transforming us into the image of Christ. This book will show how the principles of God's psychology help us find the way to health and happiness. The book is written for anyone who

- wants to know where he or she is on the self compass.
- desires a better marriage and family life.
- can't get rid of guilt feelings.
- craves constant reassurance from others.
- has a hair-trigger temper.
- always criticizes others.
- is trapped by shyness.

Jesus—the Son of God and the Son of man—is a marvelously whole person. He calls us to use God's psychology to find a similar wholeness in ourselves.

- feels lonely and withdrawn.
- is a perfectionist.
- feels superior to others.
- faces the question: Who am I?
- feels anxious around people.
- experiences bouts of depression.
- has trouble making decisions.
- wants a closer walk with God.

The great revolution that I foresee in the twenty-first century is the transformation of millions of Christians into whole persons by the power of the Holy Spirit.

The next chapter shows how God's psychology encourages us to face our rough edges and surrender ourselves to Him.

CHAPTER 2

Roughly Hewed Stones

Yea, they made their hearts as an adamant stone.

—Zechariah 7:12 KJV

Robert is a sculptor. This muscular Native American specializes in sculpting Indian figures in spiritual repose. One of his sculptures is displayed in the Smithsonian Institution.

I visited Robert's studio one sunny Saturday afternoon. The dry smell of rock dust hung in the air. Rough-hewn stones lay on tables, shelves, and corners of the floor. Red agate, white marble, and gray granite. I wondered how he could sculpt such irregular rocks into such elegant pieces.

"How do you ever make anything out of these ugly rocks?" I asked.

His brown eyes danced. Bliss suffused his face. He walked me to the outdoor storage area.

"Most people think these rocks are useless," he said, "but I see them as beautiful. They have so much potential!" He pointed to a jagged five-foot rectangular-shaped stone. "Take this red agate. I bought it in Arizona for almost nothing. It was hidden in the corner of a dealer's lot."

Robert ran his fingers over the pockmarked surface of the rock like a mother stroking her infant. "When I saw this pattern of white-and-red streaks at the top of the stone," he said, "my heart leaped. I imagined a chief's feather headdress fanning out behind his head. When I finish the sculpture, I'm going to call it *Dignity in Prayer.*

"Ever since I was a kid, I could see beneath the surface of rocks and recognize what they could become. Like this chief here." He pointed to the red agate. "I just want to set him free."

My spine tingled at the thought of Robert in his cluttered studio, falling in love with ugly rocks and transforming them into masterpieces. We walked back inside. Robert picked up a sanding tool and began touching up a sculpture of a woman's head. I was riveted by the originality of the almost completed sculpture. The woman looked alive!

Smiling while he sanded, he asked, "See how her hair is blowing out almost a foot on her left side?"

I nodded.

"This rock was another dealer reject. It had such an odd shape that no one wanted it. But when I saw that lopsided section sticking out on the left, I knew I had a wonderful piece. She's called *Wind in Her Hair.*"

He laid down the sander and wiped the dust off with a damp cloth. "Done!" he announced. Lifting the sculpture, he presented the Indian princess to me.

I felt awed leaving Robert's studio, cradling this beautiful sculpture in my arms. On the way home, I thought of the Holy Spirit: *Our heavenly Father sends the Holy Spirit to shape us into the image of Christ.*

If we surrender ourselves to God's psychology—ugly spots and all—He can gradually sculpt us into original creations, each utterly unique. There is beauty in the stone, but we've got to keep yielding to Him. We've got to trust the process.

AN EDGY DEFENSIVENESS

When I was working on my doctorate in counseling, I found out that doctoral candidates were required to complete one hundred hours of personal therapy. *This is a waste of time,* I thought. *I've got my act together, I don't need someone snooping around my personality.* Reluctantly, I arranged for an appointment with a staff psychologist.

At the end of the first session, Dr. Vandenheuval leaned back in his rocking chair. "Dan," he said, "how much do you want to know about yourself?"

I felt my chest tightening. My hands started to sweat. "What do you mean? I'm okay, aren't I?"

The doctor scratched his balding head and smiled. "Yeah, you're basically sane," he said. "But your personality needs a lot of work. You've got an undercurrent of hostility that you try to hide. But it still shows through. That inner anger will interfere with your counseling career."

"I'm not mad at anybody!" I protested through clenched teeth.

"This is what I mean. You've got an edgy defensiveness. You feel hurt and angry when I suggest that you might have a few flaws. Are you still trying to prove yourself to someone—your mother?"

My face reddened. I felt embarrassed. *What does my mother have to do with my personality?* I thought. But suddenly, I knew. I had never broken free of her. I had never faced my inner hostility about all the years she dominated me.

Over the next few months Dr. Vandenheuval gently led me through my childhood. I faced my deepest feelings. I found out I was stuck on the assertion compass point with too much aggression. Slowly, I learned how to be more vulnerable and express affection. Before God could bring out more of my potential, I had to admit that I was a rough-hewn stone with many jagged edges.

Some Christians believe we are automatically made whole and holy when we accept the Lord. I wish that were so. But most of us have found out that accepting the Lord is only the first step on the lifelong journey toward wholeness.

A pastor wrote me from India:

While reading one of your magazine articles on the self compass, I found I was stuck on the love compass point. In my church I needed everyone's approval. This interfered with preaching the whole word of God. I found that I needed to assert myself and the Holy Spirit began to help me. Now the people know that I can speak the truth in love. Through prayer and effort, I am overcoming my need to please people. It is a joy to find that God loves the real me!

PARTIAL PATTERNS OF PERSONALITY

Eight partial personality patterns block many Christians from their true potential in Christ. All eight patterns can be located on the self compass. The compass, then, is both diagnostic and therapeutic. It reveals rough edges and shows what needs polishing.

I have labeled these patterns so that they are psychologically accurate, yet easy to remember. These labels describe the pattern, not the person.

The eight partial personality patterns are exaggerated and rigid forms of functioning. They contaminate and interfere with healthy perceptions of self, others, and God. They arrest personality development and block the spiritual transformation of personality. The partial personality patterns are clinging vines, prima donnas,

bullies, con artists, wallflowers, hermits, big shots, and perfectionists (see fig. 2.1).

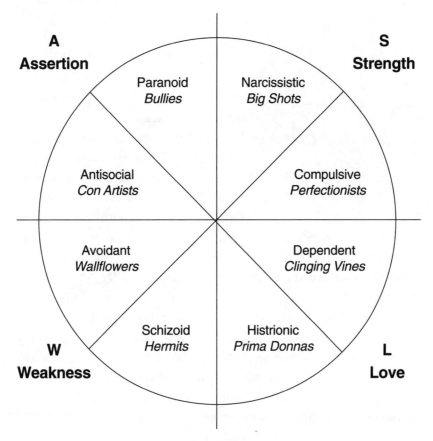

FIGURE 2.1
THE SELF COMPASS AND THE EIGHT PARTIAL PATTERNS

- Clinging vines and prima donnas are stuck on the love
  compass point. Too much love makes them compliant and
  attention craving.

- Bullies and con artists are stuck on the assertion compass
  point. Too much anger makes them abusive and exploitive.

- Wallflowers and hermits are stuck on the weakness compass point. Too much weakness makes them passive and avoidant.

- Big shots and perfectionists are stuck on the strength compass point. Too much strength makes them arrogant and self-absorbed.

> *Once we have our bearings, we can take active growth stretches.*

The self compass is a dynamic tool that allows us to find where we and others are stuck. Once we have our bearings, we can take active growth stretches. The result is gradual progress toward Christ-like wholeness. For those who need professional support in this growth, compass counseling provides a therapeutic model used in pastoral or mental health settings.

So that you can see how these rigid patterns affect every significant area of your life, we will examine each pattern from eight practical perspectives. You'll discover how positive growth stretches will help you find health and happiness in all eight areas.

Can you see yourself as a roughly hewed stone in the Master's hands? Are you willing to allow Him to set you free? If so, turn the page and continue the adventure of being sculpted by the wisdom of God's psychology.

PART 2

Partial Personality Patterns

Why do we have to spend our lives being something we would never want to be? Why do we waste our time doing things which, if we only stopped to think about them, are just the opposite of what we were made for? We cannot be ourselves unless we know ourselves. But self-knowledge is impossible when thoughtless and automatic activity keeps our souls in confusion. We cannot begin to know ourselves until we can see the real reasons why we do the things we do.

—Thomas Merton
No Man Is an Island

CHAPTER 3

Clinging Vines

Such a person can easily become overdependent on the approval and reassurance of others, or can remain indecisive, hitchhiking through life on the judgments and decisions of others.

—John Powell

Arthur became a teacher because his mother was horrified by the idea of his becoming what he wanted to be—a sculptor.

"A sculptor?" she wailed. "Whoever heard of such a thing? Nobody is looking for sculptors. Be a teacher, Arthur. Be a good boy with an honest, decent profession."

Arthur hated teaching and never got to the sculpting he so longed for. He drank more wine in the evenings than he cared to admit. He avoided fights with his wife by agreeing to whatever she wanted. Even though he went out of his way to make others happy, he was miserable. Arthur finally joined a self compass group I was leading.

In the group Arthur was open, communicative, and willing to please. Some of the group members liked his congenial ways. Others found him bland and irritating. But whenever the subject of his sculpting came up, he became animated and talkative.

"If you enjoy sculpting so much," asked Pat, "why don't you do it for a living?"

"Oh, I've thought about it a lot," said Arthur, "but it's hard to do something that'll please enough people to make the work marketable."

"Arthur," I said, "I'd like to commission you to do a bust of me in clay. You can bring it to the group when it's done, so we can get everyone's okay on it. Want to try it?"

"Sure!" Arthur replied, pleased to show off his skill. Two weeks later, he brought the clay bust to group. Looking almost breathless, he unveiled it to us. I was quite pleased with it, as was everyone else—except Martha.

"The brow is too heavy," she said.

"You're right. You're right," agreed Arthur. "I'll fix it."

But the next week Pat thought that the brow was too receding, so Arthur took it home for more work. The following week everyone but Martha thought it looked great.

"Now the chin is too sharp. You made Dr. Montgomery look like a drill sergeant," she said.

When Arthur brought his sculpture in once more, he looked dejected as he pulled off the cloth. After a few moments of silence, Donna said, "To be honest with you, Arthur, I thought it looked better the first time."

Arthur finally exploded. "What is it with you people? No matter what I do, it's not good enough. What do you want from me?"

"What do you want from us, Arthur?" I asked.

"I want you to like this sculpture. Is that too much to ask?"

"Most of us do like it," I said.

"But the idea is for you all to like it," Arthur wailed.

"What does it mean to you if everybody doesn't like it?"

"It obviously means they don't like . . . me," Arthur paused. "I'm trying to please everybody, aren't I?" He grinned sheepishly. "That's the story of my life—avoid conflict, deny anger. I'm learning something from all this."

"What are you going to do with the statue, Arthur?" I asked.

Raising both fists above his head, he brought them down onto the clay, smashing it into a formless mass. "That's what I'm going to do with it!" he roared with delight. "And when I start again—if I feel like starting again—I'm going to do it the way I please. And if any of you don't like it, that's *your* problem."

Arthur was the most surprised person in the room when spontaneously everyone cheered.

WHAT MAKES CLINGING VINES TICK?

Clinging vines strive to get others' approval by being overly submissive. They yield too often, compromise too easily, and keep their preferences to themselves. Their need for constant reassurance makes them nice to a fault.

Exaggerated love is subservient and defeating. Healthy love involves the compassion to be nurturing and supportive, yet the courage to stand up and be counted. By not actively developing their strength and assertion compass points, clinging vines come to feel hurt, depressed, and unconsciously resentful after many years of trying to please others.

This happened to Princess Diana after she married Prince Charles. At first her dream seemed to come true with a romantic, picture-perfect royal wedding. She was married to the future king of England. The dependent woman fantasizes about being swept off her feet and married to a strong man—the perfect protector and provider. But like other clinging vines, Diana was naive and easily taken in by appearances.

A few years of marriage revealed her Prince Charming to be self-absorbed, perfectionistic, and emotionally absent. She came to feel mistreated, hurt, and depressed to the point of contemplating suicide. She had lived out the dependent pattern to a tee.

Clinging vines must learn that most of their misery is self-created. They are trapped by the conditions within their own personalities—their need to make everyone happy and their unwillingness to develop emotional self-sufficiency.

I know. I spent my early thirties as a prisoner of the dependent pattern. Trying to be a good Christian led me into the pattern. I bent over backward rescuing everyone, being overly polite, and never showing irritation. The payoff was the accolades I received for being such a nice guy. Without knowing it, I'd become a dependent clinging vine.

Teaching at a Christian college, I overextended myself trying to meet everyone's needs. My Messiah complex made me volunteer to teach overload courses without pay. I counseled up to four hundred students a year, and I encouraged people to call me at home if they needed help.

Without knowing it, I'd become a servant to the endless demands of others. After three years, a secret depression developed within me that I was too embarrassed to share. I resented the smiling doormat that I'd become.

One Friday after work, an iron vise began squeezing my chest. The constriction grew tighter by the minute until I could hardly breathe. A lethargy infused my body. A fog rolled over my mind. A friend took me to an emergency room. My fatigue was so great that I couldn't lift my neck off the cot.

The doctor examined me thoroughly and announced that I was suffering from total exhaustion. He recommended an entire week in bed.

The first few days I barely had enough strength to make it to the bathroom and back to the bed. By the fourth day the fog around my mind began to lift. I thought, *I'm only thirty years old.*

How can this be happening? The answer gradually came into my awareness in the form of a voice that seemed from God.

Dan, the inner voice whispered, *you've tried too hard to please Me. You've made yourself the wrong kind of servant. You let people run over you. You've been loving others at the expense of yourself. I want you to love yourself as well as you love others.*

During that week, the Lord helped me to understand that I needed to start saying no to people's expectations and demands, that I needed a stronger sense of self-preservation. With those insights, I began moving out of the dependent pattern.

Here is what makes clinging vines tick:

1. They place their worth in other people's hands. They have an intense need for affection and approval and become anxious without both. They require constant reassurance and are upset at the slightest sign of disapproval.

2. If strong support is provided for them, they feel happy, friendly, and cooperative. But if that support waivers, they become sad and panicky.

3. They are naive and gullible, believing that all authority figures have their best interests at heart. They are imperceptive about people.

4. They want to be loved. Psychiatrist Frederick Perls writes,

If you need encouragement, praise, pats on the back from everybody, then you make everybody your judge. . . . What a dependency if you want everybody to love you! A person doesn't mean a thing to you and yet suddenly you set out and want to make a good impression on this person, to make them love you. It's always the image; you want to play the concept that you are lovable.[1]

5. They avoid growth risks and opportunities for self-sufficiency. They resist growing up and instead look to an institution or others to make their lives work.

> *Clinging vines avoid growth risks and opportunities for self-sufficiency.*

6. They fear being alone. They are bereft of an identity if no one is there to validate them.

7. They have self-doubt lurking in the basement of the psyche.

8. They mistakenly view love as a cure-all for their insecurity and fear. They are unaware that much of their suffering comes from being stuck on the love polarity and avoiding the compass points of strength and assertion.

9. They cherish the magical illusion that someone else or God will someday make them happy without risk, growth, and responsibility on their parts.

10. They are fortunate if they find a partner who has both strength and kindness. As a rule, though, they are drawn to a polar opposite: a partner who is strong and domineering, or who is aggressive and abusive.

BETWEEN MAN AND WOMAN

Clinging vines enter intimate relationships feeling unworthy at the outset. They feel lucky to find a stronger person to take care of them. Their main strategy in marriage is to subordinate themselves, so as never to offend the partner.

Growing numbers of psychologists and theologians regard diplomatic assertion as a trait in healthy marriages. Clinging vines lack this assertion compass point. Diplomatic assertion requires honest expression, self-preservation, and the power to negotiate for fairness in a relationship.

I like the definition of *assertion* provided by Robert E. Alberti and Michael L. Emmons in *Your Perfect Right.* "Assertive behavior enables a person to act in his or her own best interests, to stand up for herself or himself without undue anxiety, to express honest feelings comfortably, or to exercise personal rights without denying the rights of others."

But the clinging vine is prone to hiding behind a happy mask, repressing feelings of hurt, burying anger under a facade of duty, and ending up as a depressed and beaten-down spouse.

A Perpetual Little Girl

At a women's conference where I spoke, a fifty-year-old woman came up to me with tears in her eyes. Amy said that my discussion of the dependent style described her perfectly.

"My father always treated me like a little girl," she said, "and my mother always told me to obey him. But Dad never showed me love or affection. He just gave me orders. Then I married a man just like him. My husband doesn't ever ask what I want or need. He bosses me around and tells me I can't do anything right. What hurts the most is that my church has taught me the same thing— that I have no rights, that I'm supposed to serve everybody and never think of myself!"

I support a new trend in the Christian world in which women are neither dependent little girls nor aggressive know-it-alls. The truth is that men and women alike need whole personalities. The best marriages edify both partners, while demeaning neither. As Paul said, "There is neither male nor female; for you are all one in Christ Jesus" (Gal. 3:28).

SEX IN MARRIAGE

Clinging vines have considerable anxiety about sex. They've trained themselves not to think or speak about sexual behavior. They naively believe that if they keep their minds blank slates in sexual matters, everything will work out fine from the wedding night on. They become naive about sexual realities. They become overly dependent on the marriage partner to show them what's what. The problem is, they are so easily embarrassed that they can hardly communicate about sex, even in the marriage bed.

Sexual dysfunction can set in because clinging vines overly focus on the partner's needs. They believe that their personal pleasure is sinful and selfish.

They are prone to do whatever the more assertive partner wants, without sharing their own needs. So the sex becomes one-sided. They lose interest, yet continue to perform out of duty. Sex becomes an empty ritual.

Another unfortunate legacy is their hypersensitivity to feedback. They are deeply hurt if the partner wants to share constructive criticisms. They take the comments to mean they've failed completely and are unlovable.

THOUGHT PATTERN

All partial personality patterns engage in automatic self-talk. Self-talk is the way our brains ruminate about our life assumptions. The automatic self-talk of the clinging vine involves constant worry about what other people think.

Dependent self-talk sounds like this:

> *The automatic self-talk of the clinging vine involves constant worry about what other people think.*

- I am responsible for the happiness of others.

- I should never offend another person.

- I must keep the peace at all costs.

- I should be a good listener; my opinions don't count.

- It is selfish to think of my own needs.

- Authority figures should always be obeyed because they know best.

- Traditions should never be questioned because they make us secure.
- If I'm nice to them, others will like me.

Under the dictates of this pattern, a person should be able to endure everything, to trust everyone, to like everybody at all times.

EMOTIONAL LIFE

Clinging vines' most frequent feeling is anxiety—the fear of disapproval. They periodically experience heightened anxiety—or its opposite, deep depression—when they think someone is upset with them. This anxiety isn't limited to marriage but exists with children, coworkers, and relatives.

If their mainstay relationship is in long-term conflict, they may sink into suicidal thinking. On the other hand, whenever they receive approval or support from the partner, they experience only tenuous satisfaction because they need constant reassurance. Dependent clinging vines are bereft of an identity in their own right, which means that they keep seeking external approval.

Some dependent women become sick with worry and frustration when they can't get the approval they need from their husbands. They may learn that constantly reporting aches and pains makes their husbands more sympathetic.

Another tactic is to get pregnant when a marriage is on the rocks. The clinging vine reasons that having a baby will bind her husband to his family. She sees pregnancy as a way to get love and attention.

A dependent husband tries to marshal his wife's nurturing instincts by being needy in childish ways. He wants her to choose his clothes for him and make his decisions at home and at work. Trying to act pleasant all the time leaves a dependent husband and his wife in the dark about his true feelings.

PERCEPTION OF GOD

Clinging vines view God as a stern authority figure. He is all-powerful, all-knowing, and all-seeing: "He knows if you've been bad or good, so be good for goodness sake." They obey Him out of fear, so they won't be punished. But if you ask them, they'll say that God loves all the children of the world, and that they serve Him out of love.

They are speaking the truth to this degree: their love is the conscious part of their awareness; the fear is unconscious. Regardless of how hard they try to please Him, they don't have confidence in His unconditional love.

Underneath the Smiles

A pastor named Gordon came to see me for counseling. He had served in the ministry for fifteen years and was burning out.

"I don't know why I'm depressed," he said. "I've got a loving wife, a good teenage boy, and my ministry is successful. I get along with everybody. People like me and treat me well. But I'm terribly depressed underneath my smiles."

"It sounds like you have a good life in many ways," I said. "But I'm curious about something. How do you see God?"

Gordon's body came to attention as though a general had just walked into the room. "I should serve God at all times. I should love everyone in my church. I should never refuse a need or request."

"Wow!" I said. "Those are tall orders. Tell me, do you take on more responsibilities than you can handle so that nobody will be disappointed?"

"Yes, my wife says I get loaded down like a camel."

"Do you need constant assurance that you are doing okay, that you're a nice person?"

"Yes, I guess I do." He squirmed a bit in the black leather chair.

"One last question, Gordon. Are you on your best behavior right now so that I'll think you're a nice guy?"

Jesus draws out our potential for love, assertion, weakness, and strength. If we let Him, Jesus helps us find our way to health and happiness.

"How did you know that!" he exclaimed.

Toward the end of the session, I said, "Gordon, you've been living in the grip of the dependent personality pattern. Try reading the Gospels again. If you find times when Jesus expresses anger, think about why He was being assertive. If He refuses people's demands or frustrates their expectations, look at the reasons for His strength."

"I'm thinking right now about some passages where the Lord did these things. I never thought those Scriptures applied to me." Gordon looked thoughtfully out the window. "But I'm recalling something that seems to have my name on it."

"What's that?" I asked.

He smiled. "Jesus said, 'I don't seek people's approval or disapproval.'"

"Right on, Gordon!" I said and smiled back.

GROWTH AND CHANGE

Shawna came into counseling in an unusual way. She had been reading my book *How to Survive Practically Anything* the very weekend she had contemplated suicide. Shawna and her husband had been in San Francisco that weekend. She became so depressed that he found her trying to open the window of their seventeenth-floor suite. She wanted to jump out. I'm going to let Shawna tell her story:

When I first came into counseling, I had no idea what I felt inside myself. I was numb to my own feelings, except for a black depression. Even though I was functioning adequately at work, one of my sons said to me, "Mom, how come you don't smile or joke anymore?" Even my smile had gone, which I had pasted on for years so that I wouldn't get anyone upset or angry. I did everything I could to avoid anyone in my family expressing anger. My chief role was to make things nice for everybody.

If either of my two sons would start to fight with each other, I would walk in and separate them and say, "You have to be nice to each other." I felt that my husband's remoteness and temperamental moodiness would go away only if I could be sweet, smooth things over, and do everything that he wanted—his way.

In my first counseling session, I felt that Dr. Montgomery had X-ray vision, that he could look right inside me. When he said that my unconscious was filled with fury about holding in all of my real feelings for years, I suddenly saw the truth. A wave of relief swept over me. I felt hope for the first time. When I mentioned that I had had gall bladder surgery at thirty-five years of age, he suggested that the overeating I had done was to stuff my feelings. He said that gall is the symbol for anger and that my gall bladder had captured and stored my vile feelings until it had to be taken out—that now was the time to own all of my feelings and learn to express myself honestly.

My counseling lasted once a week for one year. The ideas about the self compass seemed to click inside me. I began to catch myself when I was swallowing a feeling I needed to express. Then I would consciously stretch from the love pole to the assertion pole and say I didn't like something, even though it might upset the person. Sometimes I went overboard into aggression, where I would verbally attack my husband or yell at the kids. At those times I learned that I could swing back into the love pole to ask forgiveness or make amends.

By the third month, my depression had lifted. I began to feel that I was a person in my own right, that I could express love, assertion, weakness, or strength without being servile and ashamed of myself. It was wonderful to no longer be held hostage to other people's opinions. My playfulness began to surface, I laughed more, and I became more sexually responsive. After decades of living with a straitjacket of steel that kept me from breathing, I finally felt self-consciousness melt away and the joy of living flow through me.

This didn't mean that I felt great all the time. In fact, I felt a full range of feelings more intensely than I ever had. Joy. Sadness. Courage. Anxiety. Self-esteem. Vulnerability. An old friend of mine who hadn't seen me during that year said that she didn't recognize me. We went out for dinner on Friday night and she said, "Shawna, you are so alive now, like you've finally come home to yourself." I knew she was right.

> *You learn to cope with life by standing on your own two feet.*

How do you outgrow the dependent pattern? By feeling more comfortable with yourself. You learn to cope with life by standing on your own two feet.

Instead of looking to others for self-worth, you define yourself as worthy: "I define myself as a worthwhile person; therefore, from now on I am a worthwhile person!" This is the new self-talk you've always needed, and God's psychology supremely supports it.

Over time this new assumption transforms dependency into autonomy. Being autonomous means you're self-governing. You follow your sealed orders from Christ. You accept that "the buck stops here." You cease blocking your intuitions and swallowing your emotions, accepting that there will be times when this is difficult. Like Jesus, you tactfully express what you feel, and you worry less about what people might think.

The truth is that you're not in the world to live up to everyone's expectations—especially since all humans are created equal in their ability to be foolish and shortsighted. Why assume that everybody else knows more than you do? Why not develop your decision-making capability instead of craving reassurance from others? Why not learn to negotiate for change instead of putting up with bad situations indefinitely? You can choose to outgrow the dependent pattern. You must take new risks to develop a self-identity that works by using the rest of your self compass.

PRACTICAL GROWTH STRETCHES

1. Clinging vines are afraid to express personal tastes, desires, and preferences. This week tell one other person about your favorite color, food, music, hobby, and book. Dare to express yourself straight out. You become more visible in the world, and people come to understand what's inside—what makes you unique.

2. Challenge your fear of making waves. In conversations with at least three people, clearly state your bias, opinion, or belief on a topic. For instance, if someone is a Republican and you are a Democrat, say so. If someone loved a movie and you hated it, say so. You must learn that you have the right to disagree without being a bad person. Practice expressing your opinions so that others can respect your point of view.

3. Carefully observe the behavior of people you know who can diplomatically express themselves without hiding, compromising, or being belligerent. Begin to internalize such models by acting the same way. Copy their healthy assertion until assertion flows spontaneously from your personality. Give yourself a test at the end of the week by tactfully negotiating for something you really want or need in a calm but firm manner.

4. Dare to handle someone's rejection or disapproval of your behavior this week by telling yourself that you are not in the world to live up to that person's expectations. Absolutely refuse to feel guilty about it. If someone points out a fault, immediately bring into your mind a strength or good point about yourself. Quit being haunted by anyone's disapproval. Ask Christ to strengthen your self-identity so that you can stand up for yourself without apology.

5. Ponder the following Scriptures and ask the Holy Spirit to reveal their unique meaning in your life. Write about your personality growth in a journal.

Don't copy the behavior and customs of this world, but be a new and different person with a fresh newness in all you do and think (Rom. 12:2 TLB).

"Learn to be wise . . . and develop good judgment and common sense! I cannot overemphasize this point." Cling to wisdom—she will protect you. Love her—she will guard you (Prov. 4:5–6 TLB).

Be wise as serpents and harmless as doves (Matt. 10:16).

Am I now seeking human approval, or God's approval? Or am I trying to please people? If I were still pleasing people, I would not be a servant of Christ (Gal. 1:10 NRSV).

I am leaving you with a gift—peace of mind and heart! And the peace I give isn't fragile like the peace the world gives. So don't be troubled or afraid (John 14:27 TLB).

For the Holy Spirit, God's gift, does not want you to be afraid of people, but to be wise and strong, and to love them and enjoy being with them (2 Tim. 1:7 TLB).

If God is for us, who can be against us? (Rom. 8:31).

6. Make an independent decision and follow through on it, no matter what. It may mean signing up for a community college class, buying something nice for yourself, joining a health spa, or resigning from a committee. Resist the temptation to ask people's opinions about your decision. The point is to take responsibility for your life and make some autonomous choices because they seem right to you.

CHAPTER 4

Prima Donnas

Let us follow the Holy Spirit's leading in every part of our lives. Then we won't need to look for honors and popularity, which lead to jealousy and hard feelings.

—Galatians 5:25–26 TLB

Doug sat in my office on the edge of his seat. The thirty-year-old trial lawyer wanted to discuss his string of failed efforts in sustaining a relationship that would lead to marriage. He complained about his on-again, off-again pattern with women.

"I treat women great at first," he said. "I buy them presents, send them flowers, and take them to fancy restaurants. I make all kinds of promises about what I can do for them. I get in way over my head. Then just when they think I'm going to pop the question, I cut and run. It's like a crazy roller coaster ride."

As he continued talking, I noticed a pattern of jumping from one subject to another, hardly stopping to breathe. "So I don't know why this always happens to me. Oh, I forgot to tell you about my new Porsche. It's candy apple red and really wows the women. But I'm not here just to talk about women. I want my whole life to get better. I even went to the doctor the other day—I had to park two blocks away; you'd think he'd have a bigger parking lot for his patients—and he said I've got some hypertension. Anyway, I don't think you can believe everything you read about stress these days. My father lived to be eighty-two. Now why was I telling you all that? But anyway, the woman I'm dating now is driving me nuts . . ."

Everything Doug was saying had to be punctuated with dramatic hand gestures and facial expressions, as though he was an actor on stage.

After about fifteen minutes of his nonstop talking, I raised my hands in the sign of a referee's time-out. "Whoa, Doug," I said. "Now it's my turn. Do you want to know the bottom line about your problems?"

"Well sure, Dr. Montgomery. But first shouldn't I tell you about my childhood? I'll never forget the day . . ."

I gave the time-out sign again. "Doug, what you're doing right now—your style of nonstop talking—is a major clue to your problems. You are stuck in the histrionic personality pattern, which means that your need for attention is so great that you must be center stage all the time. You're afraid that if you're not continually entertaining and charming others, they will lose interest in you. Does that sound right?"

"That's what I'm like all right. Anyway, just last week . . ."

I made a time-out gesture again. "Doug, I'd like you to breathe deeply and sit back in your chair. Just forget about convincing me of anything, and let me do the talking."

With that, Doug's counseling truly began. It took several months for him to let go of his emotionally pressured style of communication, to face and work through the anxiety that lay underneath. But gradually, his body relaxed, and he began to take his time in sharing his thoughts and feelings. The hardest part was learning to really listen to others.

WHAT MAKES PRIMA DONNAS TICK?

Prima donnas are extroverted individuals who see themselves in terms of their emotional impact on others. They feel an urgent inner pressure to captivate others and keep their attention. They use exaggerated facial expressions, sweeping arm motions, gimmicky laughs, and motormouth storytelling. They desire to be alluring and enchanting, but their behavior can strike others as vain, shallow, and overwhelming.

The apostle Peter is a person in the Bible who was initially histrionic before his gradual transformation by the Holy Spirit. He often acted on the spur of the moment, for example, when he cut off the ear of the high priest's servant. He expressed his emotions impetuously. He blurted out that Jesus was the Son of God, but later protested that he didn't even know the Lord. As life went on, however, Peter settled down and became a rock of stability and love. He developed wholeness and originality.

Synonyms for the word *histrionic* include *melodramatic, fickle, hammy, flamboyant,* and *overwrought.* A histrionic prima donna's conversation is filled with bursts of emotion, cornball humor, hokey antics, and a flood of unrelated ideas bridged by superficial associations.

Unlike clinging vines who are *passively* stuck on the love compass point, prima donnas *actively* pursue the approval of others through attention seeking, sexual seductiveness, eye-catching clothing, and hyped-up emotion. Histrionic prima donnas share with narcissistic big shots the search for glory. But the difference between them is that big shots disdain dependency on others, while prima donnas are extremely dependent on others for feelings of self-worth.

The following is a list of what makes prima donnas tick:

1. They see themselves as gregarious, fun loving, and fascinating. They hate it when someone suggests that they're vain, shallow, and fickle.

2. They thrive on attention and praise. If others don't say that they're the best, the brightest, and the most attractive, they'll be cut to the quick.

3. They like to be busy organizing people events all the time. The more clubs they belong to, the better. The more their names appear in newspapers, in bulletins, and on people's lips, the happier they are. The more places they go, the more excited they feel.

4. They can't stand to be left alone. They feel empty without an audience egging them on.

5. They can talk about meaningful relationships, self-identity, and career planning. But don't expect them to act on this information. They want to impress others with a show of knowledge and sincerity, but they don't expect others to hold them accountable.

> *Prima donnas love to attract attention by saying outlandish things.*

6. They love to attract attention by saying outlandish things, laughing loudly, crying hysterically, or buttonholing others about their latest agony or ecstasy.

7. In work settings they seek to keep people's attention. Actual work bores them. They would rather brag about their children, go out for lunches, check their appearance every few minutes, or go on about marital woes.

At work a histrionic charmer named Rona constantly talked about her marriage problems. She was full of stories about how her husband would mistreat her one week, and she'd receive flowers from him the next. She'd be gloomy and down in the mouth one day, and flighty and excited the next.

Finally fed up, the staff of nine coworkers confronted her with their frustration over her histrionic storytelling. Predictably, Rona rushed from the room in tears, pouted, and kept to herself the next day. And the day after, she came in with brand-new stories.

8. They can't remember people's names. They misplace car keys. They forget where they have parked. They lose their credit cards. They refuse to take responsibility for these actions; they turn them into new source material for capturing their listeners.

Prima donnas were usually spoiled as children by receiving too much attention. Praise was lavished on them for being funny or cute. They came to believe that they were the center of the universe, and that something was wrong with them if the applause stopped.

Tears of a Clown

Wendall was a twenty-year-old college student whose self-appointed role was class clown. He'd act up in my general psychology class, but the class was so large that I couldn't stop his snickering in the back. He would raise his hand now and then and set off a commotion with his off-the-wall remarks.

Around campus, Wendall constantly horsed around. Then he enrolled in my theories of personality course, a smaller class in which I typically help students see the patterns of their personalities.

The first few weeks, when I discussed Freud, Adler, Horney, and others, he continued his distracting antics. But the Monday that I lectured on the self compass—and described the histrionic personality in graphic terms—he looked white as a sheet.

The next day he sat in the front row and took copious notes for the first time. The clowning around and toothy grin were gone. He came to me after class and said that he had just seen his real self in the mirror of my lectures, and he didn't like what he saw.

I smiled and put my hand on his shoulder. "I know what you mean, Wendall. In high school I sometimes tried to be the life of the party. But when I'd look in the mirror at night before bed, I'd see an emptiness that I couldn't laugh off."

"What did you do?" he asked with a veil of tears in his eyes.

"I came to a point where I was sick of being a phony extrovert. I started thinking about some of the deeper issues of life, like you're doing. I realized that other people had a lot to offer me. You might say I took the cotton out of my ears and put it in my mouth a while. I asked God to help me settle down and get real. Over time, He did."

I observed Wendall's transformation during the rest of that year. He slowly became a calm, studious student with a bright—but no longer histrionic—sense of humor.

BETWEEN MAN AND WOMAN

Female prima donnas are drama queens, while males tend to be Casanovas. They were usually rewarded from an early age for good looks and charm rather than for competence or industry. They developed manipulative ploys for stealing the limelight. Their personalities were arrested at the level of infantile demandingness.

A hidden sense of hollowness haunts prima donnas when they are alone or are in a new place. They repress this feeling by calling friends and planning to go out. Away on a conference, one histrionic woman named Rita went out dancing with her female coworkers. She flirted with every man who came her way, and she tried to attract the men who approached her friends.

Prima donnas appear charming, friendly, and sensuous at the beginning of a relationship. But as the relationship matures, they exasperate their partners with round-the-clock needs for total attention. They bluster about, sulk, or rant and rave if they aren't constantly pampered.

They often start a marriage with exuberant energy, promising the moon and the stars. But over time, the novelty wears off. They can become bored and depressed, and they start looking for someone new.

Prima donnas must hide the negative aspects of their behavior—aggression or ambition—through denial and rationalization. They resist any awareness of their faults, pettiness, or contradictions.

No matter who we are, love and assertion and weakness and strength let us radiate our uniqueness—to be free and creative in fulfilling our destinies.

SEX IN MARRIAGE

Prima donnas are generally fascinated with sex, eroticism, and romance. They have such high-flying fantasies and expectations that a spouse may not be able to keep up. They are quite good at playing the game of sexual titillation, but they become immature and apprehensive as things get more serious.

Since prima donnas thrive on spontaneity, they love the thrill of having sex in unusual places, staging an elaborate buildup before lovemaking, or constantly coming up with something new. All this is well and good, except they have such high ideals about excitement that they become quickly bored if these expectations aren't met. The fickleness, moodiness, and petulance of prima donnas can be triggered if the partner isn't pursuing them with enough ardor or frequency.

THOUGHT PATTERN

In counseling, one man confessed, "I'm really a show-off, a cry-baby, and a windbag. But if I lose people's attention, I feel like a big nothing." Here is the automatic self-talk of the prima donna:

- I can't help forgetting things and being distractible.
- My concentration problems are not my fault.
- People like having me around because I'm such a live wire.
- Don't you think I'm fascinating?
- Let's hurry this work so we can party!
- I am irresistible and deserve special attention.
- I am intuitive and my feelings are infallible.
- Keeping people's attention makes me happy.

Whether in relationships, finances, careers, or child rearing, prima donnas prefer having magical thinking rather than dealing with facts, details, and responsibilities. Magical thinking is a naive belief that the world is there to satisfy their craving for admiration and excitement.

EMOTIONAL LIFE

Lacking substance and depth, prima donnas offer energy and excitement to others in lieu of a real self. Minor inconveniences become catastrophes. They become furious at innocent remarks, and they fall in love at first sight.

They exhibit high spirits when they are successfully entertaining other people. But when they are thwarted, their emotions change rapidly to petulance or forlornness. Ironically, their most hidden feelings are depression and self-pity.

They feel panicky if there's a silence in conversation. If a person doesn't dote on them, they can flip-flop from seeing that person as wonderful to seeing her as totally awful. They take everything personally. When they don't get their way, they try to coerce compliance by playing coy, throwing tantrums, or threatening suicide.

A man told of a scene his wife created when he tried to leave for a weekend to visit his ailing mother. The wife said that if he really loved her, he would never leave her, no matter what.

> *Prima donnas have a tendency to emotionalize or romanticize all situations and relationships.*

As he opened his car trunk to load his suitcase, she screamed out the upstairs window that she was going to kill herself as soon as he pulled out of the driveway. Under great duress, he unpacked his suitcase and went upstairs to the bedroom. Within the hour she had changed her mood. She tried to sweet-talk him into having sex since he had been such a good boy and come back to her.

Prima donnas have a tendency to emotionalize or romanticize all situations and relationships. Their life scripts read like Gothic romances—the marriage made in heaven that was suddenly shattered, the glorious opportunity that turned into disaster, the marvelous moment that was forever ruined.

The emotions of prima donnas can swing back and forth on a pendulum between love and hate, enchantment and despair, excitement and boredom. From their view, bad luck or other people's behavior is responsible for the erratic mood swings. In fact, the histrionic pattern creates impetuousness and mood swings.

PERCEPTION OF GOD

Prima donnas believe they are God's gifts to the world. They have special permission to be loud, naughty, or silly because God is so impressed with them, and they will try to become the focus of attention in any group.

Ministers with histrionic trends exhaust their congregations by constantly trying to pump everybody up. If a service isn't dramatic or emotional, or if people don't laugh their heads off or cry their eyes out, the minister may consider the service a flop.

I attended a church in which the assistant pastor seemed histrionic. Not only did he talk nonstop, but he also blew his trumpet right into the microphone to accompany the choir's special anthem. The choir director looked appalled, but the man paid no attention. He finished the selection and said, "I love playing my horn for you good people."

GROWTH AND CHANGE

A forty-year-old woman named Mandy told me that her father bought her gorgeous dresses on most holiday occasions. Her mother always told her that she was the cutest girl in the world.

Her parents hung numerous professional portraits of her on walls throughout the house.

In high school, Mandy received instant popularity for her good looks. Her makeup was always immaculate, even glamorous. She picked clothes that showed off her curves. Studies bored her, so her grades were poor. But she pursued other aims, like being elected vice president of her class, becoming a cheerleader, and dating the quarterback on the football team.

She barely got into college, but she quickly discovered she was a natural for school plays. The only difficult part was remembering her lines. Pursued by boys, she dated every weekend. Pursued by girls, she was rushed by the best sorority her freshman year. But by her junior year, boredom set in.

Mandy decided it was time to marry. She set her sights on the president of the most popular fraternity. She batted her eyes innocently, danced erotically, and swooned gracefully. On dates with him she kissed dreamily, dressed sexily, and acted coyly. Within three months he proposed. Against the parents' wishes, she dropped out of school and was married that summer.

So what was wrong with Mandy's fairy-tale existence, filled with romance, accolades, and crowning moments? To all appearances, it was a picture-perfect life, complete with Prince Charming taking her off to live happily ever after. The reality was that her histrionic personality undermined her life of perfect appearances.

During the first year of marriage, Mandy dropped her enchantress facade. Her darker side of turbulent emotions, passionate jealousy, pouty diatribes, and stifling possessiveness came out. After two more years, Prince Charming said he was sick of being married to the wicked witch of the west. He divorced her.

Now at age forty, Mandy had divorced once again. This time she became bored with her husband and fell in love with another man. But as soon as she was divorced, the other man dropped her, complaining about her temper tantrums.

When Mandy came to our first session, I told her that perhaps this could be the year she faced herself—a year set aside for personality growth. By the third session the scales had come off her eyes. She understood that her pattern had disrupted her education and two marriages. She became determined to use her pain as motivation to change.

Over the next year Mandy made excellent progress. She accepted her personality foibles, found healing for her hidden inferiority feelings, and developed a calm and effective way for communicating to others. She cut the psychological umbilical cord that had made her crave people's approval. She weaned herself from social dependencies and learned to handle and enjoy a degree of solitude. Her self-esteem no longer rose or fell based on people's reactions to her. She relaxed considerably.

Mandy is now back in college finishing a degree. Through God's psychology she is developing a whole personality.

PRACTICAL GROWTH STRETCHES

1. Accept the fact that you use emotions in exaggerated and attention-getting ways that backfire. Learn to enjoy give-and-take in conversations and to lay aside your need to stay center stage. Practice healthy self-talk:

- I need to finish telling this story and let someone else talk.
- I don't have to pour out massive energy, giving big emotional responses to whatever people are talking about.
- I can get rid of this wild laugh, and people will still like me.
- I can breathe between sentences, weighing my words and keeping my train of thought without adding irrelevant details.

2. Deliberately choose not to overload people in your first encounters. When you meet new people this week, relax and let them talk about themselves. Resist the urge to butt in with dramatic personal stories. Breathe deeply from your abdomen to counter your

anxious need to impress. Just be your real self. Practice eye contact instead of playing to an audience for laughs and special effects.

3. Get over your addiction to the superficial. Instead of trying to make life seem exciting through spreading gossip, overreacting to every little thing, and taking everything personally, go for more depth in your interactions with others. Instead of running the gamut of emotions, concentrate on the content and feeling of the one thing you are expressing, and follow it through to completion. Then pause, breathe, and relax. Accept that life is sometimes ordinary, routine, and boring.

4. How do these Scriptures relate to you? Invite the Lord to help you develop emotional stability, objective thinking, stick-to-itiveness, and serenity.

What are you so puffed up about? What do you have that God hasn't given you? And if all you have is from God, why act as though you are so great? (1 Cor. 4:7 TLB).

How long will ye love vanity? (Ps. 4:2 KJV).

They mouth great swelling words, flattering people to gain advantage (Jude 16).

[Jesus said], "You gladly honor each other, but you don't care about the honor that comes from the only God!" (John 5:44 TLB).

[Jesus said], "Beware of practicing your piety before others in order to be seen by them; for then you have no reward from your Father in heaven" (Matt. 6:1 NRSV).

Love suffers long and is kind; love does not envy; love does not parade itself, is not puffed up; does not behave rudely, does not seek its own, is not provoked (1 Cor. 13:4–5).

[Jesus said], "Do not worry about your life, what you will eat or what you will drink; nor about your body, what you will put on. Is not life more than food and the body more than clothing?" (Matt. 6:25).

[Jesus said], "Approval or disapproval means nothing to me" (John 5:41 TLB).

5. Do three things on your own this week without dramatic storytelling to anyone. Discover that you have an identity apart from other people's responses to you. Develop more of an ability for healthy solitude and independent functioning. Read a book, eat at a new cafe, take a little road trip, enjoy a sunset, or write in your journal—and keep it to yourself.

CHAPTER 5

Bullies

These . . . are constant gripers, never satisfied, doing whatever evil they feel like; they are loudmouthed "show-offs," and when they show respect for others, it is only to get something from them in return.

—Jude 16 TLB

I started out life as a gentle, curious boy. I collected stamps, flew kites, played kick the can with neighborhood kids, and raised a box turtle named Quonk Quonk.

But in the winter of my sixth-grade year, my life changed. One snowy December day I was sledding down the hill in front of my home. At the bottom of the hill a gang of boys circled me like a curtain. The leader, Jimmy, jumped into the middle of the ring and smashed me with his fists until I lay unconscious, bleeding in the snow. My face was swollen with purple welts for a week. Jimmy later killed his father with a baseball bat.

Northern New Mexico was a dangerous place when I was growing up in the late 1950s. Maybe it was a throwback to America's Wild West, where the six-shooter often was used to settle disputes. One year we had twenty-one murders, several right across from the local movie theater. That's a lot of killing for a town of fourteen thousand. I never felt very safe as a kid in Las Vegas. I was always afraid.

My best friend, Butch, lived across the alley. Butch was smart and fun. We studied together, walked to school together, and tried to look out for each other. He was the only person I relaxed around. But despite the friendship, a seething chemistry of dark emotions brewed within me.

At fifteen, I was beaten for the last time. A couple of gang members jumped me at lunch and knocked me out with brass knuckles. The next week I found the toughest boy in school. His brothers were Golden Gloves boxing champs. I asked him to teach me to fight.

We met for ten brutal sessions in the gym. The final session he landed a crushing blow to my front teeth, but I didn't go down. Something inside me snapped, like a taut rubber band. *I am not going to take this anymore, not from anyone,* I thought. I exploded with a vicious right hand that decked him. I felt the heady surge of brute power and vengeance.

Within a week I chased down one of the guys who had jumped me at lunch and I punched him out. The next day three of his buddies cornered me in an alley. I beat the leader to a pulp. The others ran.

Suddenly, I wanted to fight anyone who looked at me crosswise. When my Latin teacher threatened to send me to the principal's office for acting up in class, I promised to destroy his car if he did. He backed down and I felt powerful. I no longer wanted to just protect myself; I wanted to *prove* myself.

One night when I was sixteen, I invited a group of kids to my house for a party. Butch and I made punch and sandwiches. I danced with Marcia, my girlfriend. Then some uninvited older

*If we surrender
ourselves to God's
psychology—ugly
spots and all—
He can gradually
sculpt us into
original creations,
each unique and
beautiful.*

boys came in. One was Monty, a neighbor and the center on our football team.

I told Monty and his friends to get lost. Monty looked at me, surprised. That look was all it took. I decked him and then followed up with a flurry of blows while he lay helpless on the floor. It took three boys to pull me off. Butch and Marcia looked on in horror as Monty's friends carried him to their car. Monty took a half-dozen stitches in his face at the hospital.

Well, I rationalized, *if I don't stick up for myself, who will?* Yet deep inside I was shaken. Monty hadn't done anything to deserve that vicious attack.

I started drinking on the weekends. That was like dousing a fire with gasoline. One Saturday night I was returning from a hunting trip with some friends. We came up on a motorcycle with two riders, a couple of toughs who had beaten up on me in junior high.

I shouted to Bobby, who was driving, "Pull up next to them!" Then I thrust my shotgun out the window just a few feet from the driver's head. He looked at me in horrified recognition. I was glad he knew why I was pointing that gun at him. I pulled back the hammer and aimed at his face. Then I pulled the trigger. But not before raising the barrel about three inches above his head.

The blast sent them flying off the road and spinning into a ditch where they cursed us as we roared off.

I was out of control. My parents were called into the principal's office to hear about my drinking. My friends were deserting me, all except Butch. Then one night I turned on him.

We argued at a party. Butch left in a car with some friends. I went berserk. Fear, betrayal, rage. I jumped in my car in hot pursuit, the speedometer breaking a hundred. I caught up with them on Seventh Street and cut them off at a stop sign. Adrenaline poured through my body as I jumped out of my car and ran around to the passenger side where Butch was sitting. He didn't have time to roll up the window. I pummeled him. Some of my blows landed wildly on the steel frame of the window, shredding my knuckles. Yet I felt no remorse. To this day I can recall the look of confused fear on Butch's face as I hit him again and again.

I'd lost my best friend, and there was no one to blame but myself. I felt terrible. *You've got to control your temper,* I told myself. *You're turning into a maniac.* I resolved to straighten up. And for a while life went smoothly. Then in the fall of my senior year, Marcia broke up with me and started dating Mike, the new guy in town. I wanted to kill him.

Mike threw a huge party at the Castanada Hotel ballroom. Everyone was invited. Except me. I got drunk, then drove over to the party. I made my way to the door and demanded in. When the chaperones asked to see my invitation, I went crazy.

I screamed at Mike over the arms and bodies of parents who were desperately trying to restrain me, "Come out and fight like a man!" All the kids stopped dancing and peered at me. Vodka and the urge for revenge made me feel like I could fight them all. Only when one of the parents started to phone the police did I back off. Still in a blind fury, I jumped in my '57 Chevy and peeled out, tires screaming, radio blaring.

Deep in my heart I hated what I'd become. I never laughed or smiled. I wore a poker face and a mean stare meant to keep people away. I was digging a deeper and deeper hole for myself, and there seemed to be no way out.

Four nights after threatening Mike at the party, I was walking home with a half pint of vodka stuffed in my old leather jacket. The coolness chilled my face. I passed an old Methodist church on the corner of University and Eighth Streets. As I stood at the stoplight, singing reached my ears. I didn't like churches. But something lingered around me for a moment—a friendliness that seemed to have come from the church, beckoning me through the big double doors.

I hesitated. *What will people think if I go in? I have a reputation around town. No way I'm going in there.* But the tug on my heart gently strengthened. I turned, walked up the stairs, and opened the door. I couldn't believe that I was walking into a Wednesday night church service.

Several people recognized me and looked surprised. I sat down in the nearest seat. My face heated up. I was blushing. But before long I noticed something else. I felt strangely welcomed. The friendliness that I had felt out on the street seemed more personal.

The minister was talking about Jesus. He said that Jesus was considered by some religious people of His day to be a rebel and a rabble-rouser, a friend of sinners. I could relate to that. The minister said that Jesus is alive today, and that He can enter a person's heart and give him peace.

I felt a need for God, but at the same time I questioned His existence. I was aware of an incredible emptiness inside me, a longing so deep that I had no words for it. I didn't know how to connect to God. Could somebody show me? At the end of the service I went up to the altar and knelt.

The minister asked my name, then asked, "Would you like me to show you the plan of salvation?" I felt some reluctance, but I nodded my head. He opened his Bible to several passages that showed me my need for Christ:

For all have sinned and fall short of the glory of God (Rom. 3:23).

For the wages of sin is death (Rom. 6:23).

For God so loved the world that He gave His only begotten Son, that whoever believes in Him should not perish but have everlasting life (John 3:16).

But as many as received Him, to them He gave the right to become children of God, to those who believe in His name (John 1:12).

I liked that he took his time and let me read the verses for myself.

He asked if I wanted to ask Jesus into my heart as my Savior. I paused for a long moment. Then I asked, "Does this mean I have to stop drinking and fighting?"

He looked shocked. Then he smiled and said, "It means that Jesus will be your best Friend. You take it from there."

I was intrigued. I agreed to let him pray for me. He said, "Father, please accept Dan's willingness to accept Jesus in his heart and follow wherever You lead. Please show him Your great love. Always be with him." After he prayed, he asked if I wanted to pray, too. I felt embarrassed but decided to try. At the age of seventeen I said my first prayer aloud: "God, thank You for coming into my life."

As I stood, tears soaked my eyes. Warm sensations flooded my body. I felt a peace so incredible that it filled the emptiness of only minutes before. I knew that God had found me. His love seemed to cover me as I slept that night.

The next morning I opened the front door to head to school. Mike was walking by on the other side of the street. I grabbed my books and ran out of my house toward him. When he saw me coming, he threw down his books and squared off. "Are you going to bust me up?" he yelled.

"No," I said. "Something happened last night. I accepted Jesus into my life. I want to be friends."

He frowned and eyed me carefully, then bent down to pick up his books. He came back up with a smile on his face. "Okay, Danny," he said. "You may be nuts, but you're not a liar." He reached out and shook my hand.

By the end of the year, I had led fifteen fellow students and one teacher to Christ, although several of my former friends rejected me. I felt great remorse toward people I had harmed, and I made amends where I could—all except for Butch, my best friend. I figured that what I had done to him was too horrible to forgive. I felt too ashamed to apologize. After graduation, I lost track of Butch.

But I had nightmares about Butch for thirty years. Recently, the still, small voice of the Lord seemed to ask me if I was willing to make amends to Butch. I assured God that Butch hated my guts and never wanted to hear from me again.

The next day my mother called me from my hometown. "Hi, Dan," she said. "How are you doing?"

"Fine, Mom."

"Do you remember your old friend, Butch?" she said.

"Yes," I said.

"Well, his mother just told me that he recently moved to your town. You two should have lunch and talk about old times!"

With fear and trembling, I called Butch to make a luncheon appointment. He sounded reserved, but he agreed to meet me the next day.

We met for brunch, and the waitress ushered Butch to my table. He was much larger than I remembered. We exchanged small talk. Then he looked at me with eyes narrowed. "What do you want, Danny?"

Tears came to my eyes. I took a deep breath. "Butch, do you remember when I attacked you in high school?"

"Of course, I remember!" he replied. "You almost put me in the hospital!"

"Well, I want to apologize. You were the best friend I ever had. I am so sorry that I turned on you. I've had nightmares about it for thirty years. Can you possibly forgive me?"

To my astonishment, Butch broke into the old boyish smile I knew so well. He reached out, and we vigorously shook hands.

He said, "I don't hold it against you, Danny."

We left the restaurant giving each other big hugs instead of a face full of fists.

To this day I am thankful that Jesus set me free from my paranoid bully prison. Jesus—and God's psychology.

WHAT MAKES BULLIES TICK?

Anyone who is functioning from the paranoid personality pattern takes an aggressive approach in relationships. I refer to people who employ this pattern as bullies because they specialize in hurting and tyrannizing others. The paranoid leader browbeats, coerces, and dominates others. The paranoid spouse ranges in behavior from intimidating to terrorizing, from humiliating to inflicting physical abuse. The paranoid teacher rides herd over students instead of encouraging or inspiring them.

I had such a teacher in high school. She scared us all to death. Mrs. Collins barked out assignments, humiliated students right and left, and threw a number of kids—including me—out of the classroom. She'd get outraged if someone wasn't paying total attention. Believe me, there was no cross talk or humor in her class. Senior English seemed like a prison sentence.

This paranoia can exist at an institutional level as well, with the regimes of Stalin and Hitler as extreme examples. Notable paranoid bullies who have developed religious cults include the Reverend Jim Jones in Guyana and David Koresh in Waco, Texas.

Christianity is not exempt from paranoid types. Some clergy foster paranoid thinking in their congregations. They teach their flocks to be suspicious of outsiders, to hate those who are different, to argue against anything but their view, and to lambaste Christians of other persuasions. Such paranoid leaders demand total obedience from their members and wage militarylike campaigns against all perceived opposition—in God's name, of course.

A huge proportion of children's television cartoons are loaded with paranoid bully characters. I've wondered if part of the wave of national violence in the 1990s isn't related to television and movies outdoing themselves in portraying paranoid bullies.

In my work as a clinical consultant to Head Start, I've been amazed by the increase in paranoid trends among four- and five-year-old boys. One four-year-old bully whacked another kid in the eye with a block. Blood gushed out, and the kid was rushed to an emergency room. A teacher questioned the boy who acted violently. He retorted, "Nobody messes with me!"

> *Bullies are stuck on the assertion compass point with an exaggerated sense of spite and aggression in their daily functioning.*

Bullies are incapable of sustaining a warm or cooperative relationship with anyone. They are stuck on the assertion compass point with an exaggerated sense of spite and aggression in their daily functioning. They lack humility from the weakness pole, kindness from the love pole, and self-esteem from the strength pole.

The following characteristics are typical of paranoid bullies:

1. They stay in control by making mountains out of molehills, launching arguments when people least expect it, and flying off the handle to get their way. They hold grudges for years.

2. They intimidate others with icy glares, raised eyebrows, pointed fingers, cold shoulders, and long lectures. They're capable of physical violence when their rage is out of control. When they abuse others, they are convinced that others made them do it.

3. They are stubborn and proud of it. Their views are always right. Criticize them and they get meaner. Threaten them and they get stronger.

4. They can browbeat someone from a thousand miles away through a nasty letter or telephone call. They are masters of insults, barbed-wire teasing, and snide remarks. They fill people with self-doubt wherever they go. If others dare to feed back how belligerent their behavior really is, they stop them in their tracks with a double-barreled verbal blast.

5. They are outspoken about their opinions, positions, and demands on others. They believe in control, not love. They use

words of love to make people depend on them, but once others are hooked, they desire undisputed power.

6. They will go to any lengths—lose a marriage, alienate children, and destroy a career—to avoid facing that their own out-of-control anger is their real downfall.

7. They feel vindictive triumph when they defeat others.

In counseling, one forty-year-old client named Jill became aware of her mother's paranoid pattern. For a good part of Jill's life, she had felt afraid and tense around her mother, but she had never known why. She was finally able to put into words the dynamics of her mother's paranoid pattern and how it had affected her:

My mother saw herself as loving, generous, and even fun to be around. Indeed, she could be this way with people outside the family. But when alone with me she was mostly bossy and downright disagreeable.

I could never hold a conversation with her because she would talk *at* me. When I would try to express myself, she would automatically disagree with whatever I said, and get more intense about the rightness of her own view. If I persisted in trying to make a point, she would escalate into an angry diatribe to overpower me. The self compass helped me realize that Mother was stuck in the paranoid pattern.

I reached out to my father for emotional support in my teenage years and early twenties, but Mom would attack him if he expressed support for me. Dad was a rather demure man who wanted no conflicts with his wife. Sometimes he'd give me a sympathetic look and say something like, "Well, that's your mother." But most of the time he ventilated anger toward me that Mom had dumped on him.

The sad result was that my own mother became my biggest obstacle in accepting myself and in finding God's will. She undermined my friendships, criticized my relationship with God, opposed my choice of a husband, fought my choice of a career in nursing, and made doomsday predictions that if I didn't do things her way, I would surely fail.

For years I attempted to talk to my mother about her critical ways, but when I would bring up the topic, she'd explode into angry denial. Somehow there was a family rule that nobody could talk to Mom about her actual behavior. The second rule was that everything was supposed to be just fine. I can still hear her screaming, "I am not disagreeable! I am not mad!"

In order to grow psychologically and spiritually, I'm having to do two things. First, I'm giving up my need for her approval, since it will never be forthcoming. Second, I'm giving up my need to make her happy. Making her happy is impossible!

I am now finding a greater freedom to be my own person despite Mom's chronic discontent.

BETWEEN MAN AND WOMAN

In dating and mating, paranoid bullies and dependent clinging vines often attract each other like magnets but for all the wrong reasons. It is an ill-fated attraction with disastrous outcomes.

Among Hollywood marriages, Richard Burton demonstrated paranoid trends in his relationship with Elizabeth Taylor. His alcoholism fueled his verbal and physical aggression. The relationship finally exploded into a nasty divorce, but the couple couldn't get over their attraction to each other. Their romance was rekindled, and they remarried. But the remarriage did nothing to alter Burton's paranoid pattern, and by then, Taylor had also developed an aggressive and assaulting style. They divorced again after four short months, casualties of the paranoid legacy.

Many married men internalize the paranoid view that their wives and children are their private property, that they can do with them what they please, and that anger is the best way to keep family members in line.

A mark of this bullying pattern is insane jealousy. Bullies interpret any sign of independence—such as going to the grocery store without them—as indisputable evidence of disloyalty. They'll ask spouses trick questions, interrogate them relentlessly and, no matter what spouses say, conclude that they are guilty. Naturally, such behavior isolates a partner from normal social interaction, which is exactly what the bully wants to do. Bullies do not seek intimacy in marriage. They seek absolute control.

A female client said, "I can't stand for my husband to be out of my sight. I call him at work several times a day. I make sure he doesn't join anything. I watch his eyes whenever we're out together. I'm making sure he'll never be unfaithful." The same woman admitted to having an affair in their marriage. She was projecting her infidelity onto her husband, as a bully is prone to do.

A Bully's True Colors

I remember counseling Rudy, a man of forty who had come to me because his wife threatened to leave him if he didn't. His arrogance made it hard to build rapport, but after six or so sessions, Rudy finally owned up to the mind games he played with Nicole.

Nicole was a talented woman who had just finished her master's degree, worked out regularly to keep in shape, and was a fine homemaker. I asked Rudy to tell me straight out why he dished out constant criticisms of Nicole and never complimented her.

Rudy took a deep breath. Then he said,

It's true. Nicole is a beautiful and intelligent woman. She keeps the house immaculately. She is a great wife and mother. She worked very hard to get her master's degree. But I know that if I compliment her on those things, it will go right to her head. She's stupid enough to be conned into sex with some jerk. I can't let that happen. I've got to protect her. Nicole belongs to me!

I put her down for her own good. I tell her she's ugly, dumb, and selfish so that she won't get any ideas about ever leaving me. I married her because I wanted a blank slate to write my life on. I don't want her to change. If I keep her on a yo-yo, she never has time to think of anything but me.

Bullies place others in a no-win situation. They are usually quite charming during the introductory phase of a relationship, that is, until they exact a strong commitment of love. But once they enter into marriage, their surface affability quickly deteriorates into displays of anger. They put the burden of loving on spouses and constantly criticize them for not doing everything demanded. Like a pirate ship with its skull and crossbones, they hoist their true colors.

Their irritability, impatience, and spite spill out. They constantly test spouses' loyalty by stepping up their abuse to see how much spouses can take. They make ever greater demands that no one can fulfill. If spouses confront them with their unfairness, they say spouses are selfish and disloyal. However, if spouses submit to them, they become bored and intensify their abuse to entertain themselves.

> *Bullies are experts at emotional blackmail.*

Paranoid bullies are experts at emotional blackmail, and if spouses start to walk away from the relationship, they threaten to ruin their spouses or take the kids away.

Often the first show of a bully's willingness to change comes when a spouse has enough courage to say and mean, "That's enough! I won't stand for one more episode of anger, suspicion, or accusation. If you don't immediately seek help through prayer and psychological counseling, I'm leaving."

SEX IN MARRIAGE

Bullies find it almost impossible to enjoy healthy sex. They have no interest in bringing satisfaction to the partner and can feel threatened if the spouse enjoys sex too much or wants to try something new. "Where did you get that idea?" they'll ask. "Are you having sex with someone else?" they'll accuse.

In other words, bullies use sexuality as another arena for being suspicious, contrary, and antagonistic. If spouses tell them what would heighten sexual pleasure, they'll be sure not to do it or start an argument over it. Spouses have no rights with bullies. They want to decide when, where, and how often sex will occur.

In addition, many bullies don't experience arousal that comes from being attracted to the spouse or sharing emotional closeness. They have a need for a mental game, for example, insisting on sex when spouses aren't in the mood or getting pleasure from giving spouses pain.

Other paranoid mind games include ordering spouses to dress seductively in public and then interrogating them about whether they were turned on or not, making them undress in front of an open window, or bragging about the sexual attractiveness of other people to make their spouses feel insecure.

THOUGHT PATTERN

What characterizes the mental life of bullies? Their self-talk runs along these lines:

- Other people can't be trusted because they're out to deceive me.
- I must constantly test those around me to see if they are loyal.
- I'm a very important person, but no one gives me my due.
- I am stubborn and proud of it.
- If people seem friendly, they're only trying to manipulate me.

- If people seem distant, it proves they're out to get me.

- Get other people before they can get to you.

- My spouse and children are my private property—I own them.

Bullies are in denial about their harshness, cruelty, and immaturity. They see themselves as intelligent and perceptive. They justify being hard-nosed and authoritarian because people can't be trusted. They rationalize mistreatment of others as being "for their own good."

The most obvious defense mechanism to block responsibility for their aggressive personality style is projection. Bullies consider themselves righteous and well-intentioned. Others are mean, treacherous, and out for themselves.

EMOTIONAL LIFE

If you know what to look for, people trapped in the bully personality pattern give themselves away. They have a chip on the shoulder and dare you to knock it off. They are always right and launch into an argument if you express another view. They are edgy and quick to take personal offense.

> *The bully's emotional sport is batting people against the wall.*

When they are not acting in anger, bullies are sullen, tense, and restless. They are constantly ready to blame and attack. They suspect the worst about you and are quick to undermine your self-confidence.

The bully's emotional sport is batting people against the wall. People who do not understand this trait can be driven crazy by it. The bully will become bored if a relationship is peaceful, cynical if love is being expressed, and restless if communication is flowing naturally. They feel out of control and will disrupt trust, sabotage sincerity, and blow up over nothing to reestablish domination.

One bully explained it this way: "When I was a kid, I always liked to bat balls against the wall. They'd bounce back, and then I would hit them harder and harder. That's what I do to people. I get them all upset, and then I bat them around. It makes me feel powerful, like I can defeat everybody but nobody can defeat me."

Key emotions that are lacking in the bully pattern include sympathy for people in need, desire for intimacy, and remorse over hurting others. Bullies excuse their abuse of other people by saying, "They deserved it," or "They made me do it."

Deep down, bullies feel overlooked and cheated by life. They feel justified being cynical about human nature and abusing anyone who lives under their influence.

PERCEPTION OF GOD

Some years ago I met with a group of Protestant ministers and Catholic priests. A desire to bridge the centuries-old gap between these two major traditions of the Christian faith had inspired the monthly meetings. I was all for it.

People made presentations with care and diplomacy. Some of the topics included the nature of salvation, the respective roles of the Bible and the church in the Christian's life, and the role of the Holy Spirit in the world today.

A large Catholic church was selected as the site of the tenth session. The topic was the Holy Spirit in our daily lives.

Electricity charged the air as everyone gathered in the rectory for the meal and presentations. The bishop of the diocese and the pastor of the largest Protestant church in the state were the two guest speakers.

After a delightful lunch prepared by the sisters, the bishop spoke first. A distinguished gentleman in his sixties, he made sensitive and intriguing comments about the Holy Spirit.

Then all eyes turned to the Protestant minister, who stood up and walked to the podium. The middle-aged minister adjusted his glasses, firmly grasped his Bible in his right hand, and said, "If you Catholics are finally ready to admit that the Holy Bible is the only authoritative revelation of God to the human race, and if you are ready right now to receive Jesus Christ as your personal Savior, we have something to talk about. For centuries you have blasphemed the Holy Spirit with your hardness of heart and your Mary worship. If you will get on your knees and ask Jesus into your hearts, I will pray for you. If not, I don't see any point in staying any longer!"

An icy silence thicker than a fog rolled into the room. I shuddered. We were all speechless.

Then the pastor walked out.

As I've reflected on this experience over the years, I've realized that the pastor was not an evil man, just a man with a skewed self compass. He wanted to represent Christ through strength and assertion, but he lacked humility and love. Stuck as he was in the paranoid pattern, he could not respect other people's feelings and points of view. Without empathy and openness, he left the meeting with the illusion that he had outsmarted the Catholics, beat them to the punch, and scored a mighty victory for God.

Bullies are convinced that God is secretive and out to get those who are plotting against Him. They align themselves with a God who is merciless and vindictive. Bullies believe that God needs them to carry out witch hunts among the faithful and to wage war against unbelievers. Their God is filled with wrath.

Bullies don't experience the grace or love of God because their pride and need to be in control won't allow for it. Paranoid bullies end up being divisive within the body of Christ and abrasive to the world. Like Saul, they are always blaming and bashing someone.

In the Old Testament, King Saul had paranoid trends. He was arrogant beyond belief, insanely jealous of David, and abused his relationship with God by oppressing people instead of serving them. He was tormented by inner anger and capable of plotting the cold-blooded murder of David with no remorse.

Some Christian television megaministers with paranoid trends have taken hard falls. Other paranoid individuals are obsessed with attacking fellow Christians for not holding their view of God.

GROWTH AND CHANGE

Is it possible for someone stuck in the paranoid pattern to grow and change? Yes. Even for bullies there is beauty in the stone. But the catch is that you may not be motivated for personality growth precisely because you're so self-justifying: "I'm not really a bully—people just make me mad." "I'm not really stubborn and obnoxious—people just get me all riled up." "I'm not really abusive—I'm just trying to be honest."

To outgrow paranoid trends, you need to

- challenge your cynicism.
- make amends to those you've hurt or harmed.
- honestly admit your shortcomings.
- consider anger a luxury you cannot afford.
- ask for help when you need it.
- handle people's criticisms without defensiveness.
- appreciate individual differences.
- grow in tolerance, patience, and compassion for yourself and others.
- choose to trust others and give them the benefit of the doubt.
- learn to focus on God's love and mercy.

Nathaniel came across as verbally aggressive with his wife, secretary, and office workers. Because of his top dog style of relating to me, I surmised he might be stuck in a bullying approach to life.

As a chief hospital administrator, Nat prided himself on making people walk on eggshells. "When I crack the whip, people jump!" he said.

I suggested to Nat that his bullying ways were costing him dearly. His wife had become emotionally distant and sexually disinterested; he had to hire three different secretaries within a year; his fellow office workers hated him. His success had been bought at a dear price indeed.

Nat defended himself: "Everybody's a slacker at work. If I don't chew them out, they'll take advantage of me. As for my wife, she just wants an easy ride. I've got to stay on her case to keep her in line."

I used an indirect approach with Nat to make him aware of his unhealthy attitudes. He bragged about how people were afraid of him. I reframed this: "You like to see people grovel because they're afraid you'll blow your stack."

He spoke about special privileges he took at the hospital. I said, "You like to lord it over everyone."

He mentioned how he had ripped his secretary apart that very day. "You feel powerful when you make mountains out of molehills," I said.

Nat began to be irritated with these reflections. He said, "Dr. Dan, you're painting a picture of me that isn't exactly pretty. What are you getting at?"

"Nat, I'm mirroring what you're saying about yourself."

"So what's the bottom line?" he asked, taking out a handkerchief to wipe the sweat off his hands.

"I prefer that you tell me."

"That I'm a jerk?" Nat offered.

"Excellent," I said. "That's the most accurate statement you've made in one month of counseling!"

Nat struggled with the process of becoming more whole for months. Yet, he made discernible progress. A year later, his wife told me of her happiness with Nat's hard-earned turnaround. The office workers threw a surprise party for their boss. One woman said, "Nat, you've changed so much. You're not a troll anymore."

PRACTICAL GROWTH STRETCHES

1. Smash the illusion once and for all that your anger is healthy or necessary. It is neither. Your anger is your worst enemy. It threatens to destroy friendships, family, career, and your responsiveness to God.

Stop yourself five times this week when you start to get hot under the collar. Keep your mouth shut, and tell yourself that you are becoming a sensitive person who can hear and handle other people's views, feelings, and behavior.

Take several deep breaths to calm yourself down, and pray immediately for God to help you move into tolerance, forgiveness, or de-escalation. End the conversation on a friendly and positive note that demonstrates you are finally growing up.

2. Make amends to two people whom you have judged, abused, and attacked with your anger. Simply say from your heart that you now wish to give up anger and aggression as your major ways of coping with life.

Ask if they are able to forgive you. If they are at that moment, experience the grace of forgiveness. If they are not, give them time. At least you are doing your part in promoting healthy change in yourself. They will come around in good time, especially when they realize you are no longer blowing your stack.

3. Face the reality of your emotional isolation and the secret inferiority that has caused it. Talk to a friend or a professional counselor about any painful times while growing up, especially times when you felt humiliated, abused, or controlled by a family member.

Opening up creates bridges of trust to others and counters your tendencies to distrust and burn bridges. Learn to talk freely about your anxieties and weaknesses. Trust people at home or at the office, and give them space to be themselves.

Compliment people for their own style of doing things. Support them in their creative approaches to life. Work with people instead of feeling superior to them. If you start becoming suspicious and spiteful, stop in your tracks and pray for the Holy Spirit to remove your paranoia and give you a more trusting outlook.

4. Ponder the following Scriptures and give the Holy Spirit permission to help you develop a more honest self-appraisal and deeper faith in God's love and grace for you.

> A violent tempered person will pay the penalty;
> if you effect a rescue, you will only have to do it again (Prov. 19:19 NRSV).

> A soft answer turns away wrath,
> But a harsh word stirs up anger (Prov. 15:1).

> When you follow your own wrong inclinations your lives will produce these evil results . . . hatred and fighting, jealousy and anger, constant effort to get the best for yourself, complaints and criticisms, the feeling that everyone else is wrong (Gal. 5:19–20 TLB).

> And now a word to you parents. Don't keep on scolding and nagging your children, making them angry and resentful. Rather, bring them up with the loving discipline the Lord himself approves (Eph. 6:4 TLB).

> For your anger does not produce God's righteousness (James 1:20 NRSV).

> You may as well know this too, Timothy, that in the last days it is going to be very difficult to be a Christian. For people will *love only themselves* and their money; they will be *proud and boastful,* sneering at God, disobedient to their parents, *ungrateful* to them, and thoroughly bad. They will be *hardheaded* and *never give in to others;* they will be constant liars and *troublemakers* and will think nothing of immorality. They will be *rough and cruel,* and *sneer at those who try to be good.* They will betray

their friends; they will be *hotheaded,* puffed up with pride, and prefer good times to worshiping God. They will go to church, yes, but they won't really believe anything they hear. Don't be taken in by people like that (2 Tim. 3:1–5 TLB, italics mine).

So far as it depends on you, live peaceably with all (Rom. 12:18 NRSV).

5. This week be generous to a fault. Give a gift without needing or expecting repayment. Fulfill a promise joyfully. Remember someone's birthday, anniversary, or graduation by sending a nice card. Discover the pleasure of being a positive person.

CHAPTER 6

Con Artists

These six things the LORD hates, . . .
A proud look,
A lying tongue, . . .
A heart that devises wicked plans,
Feet that are swift in running to evil,
A false witness who speaks lies,
And one who sows discord among brethren.

—Proverbs 6:16–19

Dr. S. was an ambitious young psychiatrist with a thriving practice who wanted to share my office with me. He seemed friendly and professional. I agreed. I liked his gift of gab and his boisterous, off-the-wall humor.

I really enjoyed the first month of our association. Dr. S. would come bouncing into the clinic, brimming with energy and cracking jokes. But by the second month his happy-go-lucky smile waned. He came to my office and said that the IRS was giving him problems. Could I pay his portion of the month's rent? He said he would pay me back the following month. I ended up paying the total rent for that month and for each month throughout the next year. Dr. S. kept promising that I was first on his list for reimbursement, and that a large amount of money was due him any day from clients' insurance claims.

In our third month together, Dr. S. asked if he could try out one of the personality assessments that I used with my clients: "I'd like to borrow your computer scoring code so I can score one test. I'll pay you for it next week."

Since I was used to trusting professional colleagues, I said okay. Months later I was socked with a huge bill from the testing company. Dr. S. had ordered and processed twenty of the expensive tests under my name. When I confronted him, he denied it, saying that the company had to be at fault.

In the meantime, he'd borrowed another of my computer codes, this time to try out a national bulletin board to which I belonged. He promised he'd use it just once to see if he wanted to join. For the next six months I thought my modem was on the blink because the bulletin board would not open in response to my code.

After many calls and letters to that company, I finally found out that Dr. S. had replaced my code with a new one so that he could bill numerous transactions to my account without my knowledge or consent. When I confronted him, he protested that he would never do such a thing, and that the company had obviously made a mistake. He sounded so sincere that I questioned my judgment.

Other incidents cropped up. In our final month together, I noticed that several objects from my office were missing, and that my umbrella and briefcase were no longer in the office storeroom. When I mentioned these items to Dr. S., he said that we must have been robbed over the weekend, although nothing of his was missing. Later, I glimpsed my briefcase, tattered and torn, in his car trunk.

The worst was yet to come. Dr. S. said that insurance companies were giving him trouble, and that he was going to declare bankruptcy. He said that the twelve thousand dollars he owed me was going to be written off. I was dumbfounded that he felt no remorse about the situation. The last straw came when I glanced at a pile of insurance billings on his desk and saw that he'd been grossly overbilling his clients. When I confronted him, he blew up and vehemently denied any wrongdoing. He was furious that I no longer trusted him.

That week I dissolved our association, and I found a new office. Dr. S. wrote a vicious letter to me accusing me of being a disloyal friend. He wondered how I could leave him when he had been such a great colleague.

Dr. S. helped me learn firsthand that antisocial con artists are wolves dressed in sheep's clothing. Their primary goal in life is to live parasitically off others.

> *Con artists' primary goal in life is to live parasitically off others.*

WHAT MAKES CON ARTISTS TICK?

Con artists are charming and sociable on the surface but ruthless and calculating underneath. They are stuck on the assertion pole. They take advantage of people's trust or love. Their hidden agenda in all relationships is the thrill of the con and the shameless pursuit of gratification.

The antisocial pattern shares with the paranoid pattern a bent toward anger and suspicion. But con artists are more self-assured than bullies. They are streetwise, glib, and able to lie without blinking an eye. They are masters at pulling the wool over your eyes.

Antisocial Origins

Mild forms of the antisocial personality are encouraged and rewarded in our competitive society. How many of these sayings have you heard?

- Be tough, hardheaded, and realistic.
- Don't buckle under to the competition.
- When the going gets tough, the tough get going.
- Winning isn't everything; it's the only thing.
- There's a sucker born every minute.
- Get rich quick.

Boys and men are especially hard hit by antisocial enculturation. Some initiations into letterman's clubs, college fraternities, and military organizations subject young men to humiliating rituals designed to thicken their skins and harden their hearts. By wiping out young men's love and weakness compass points—so the reasoning goes—we make them strong and able to fend for themselves.

Con artists develop in abusive homes as well, where children are exploited or not respected, or where they are taught criminal ways.

Whatever the origin, con artists lose their spiritual sensitivity and feeling for humanity. They lose their ability to reverse roles with others, which results in a lack of empathy or compassion. This leads to an incredible capacity for cruelty. They experience a thrill in getting away with murder.

The Finger of Evil

My initiations into the varsity letterman's clubs in both junior high and high school were classic studies in antisocial dehumanization. While some forms of social "hazing" have since been challenged and corrected, my high school initiation was brutal. Two athletic coaches supervised it. On a Friday night, those of us who had lettered in sports were put through three hours of torture.

First, we were blindfolded and stripped naked. Then our body hair was shaved off with barber's electric clippers. Seniors used heavy-duty cattle prods to hit vulnerable parts of our bodies with high voltage. They rubbed a deep-heating ointment on our genitals and under our armpits. It burned like fire, but we couldn't scream or complain.

We were made to run a gauntlet the length of the gym floor while veteran lettermen on both sides of us swatted us as hard as they could with brooms. We had to sit on ice, eat bananas from toilets, and swallow Tabasco sauce with raw eggs. Finally, at the end of the initiation, they poured molasses over us and forced us to roll around in sawdust.

I left at midnight feeling degraded and abused, as though the finger of evil had touched my very soul. Yet I was supposed to be proud that I was a part of the world of aggressive, antisocial men.

The fact that both coaches attended my local church helped me realize that Christians are not immune to the antisocial pattern.

Here are the characteristics of con artists:

1. They disregard social rules, ethics, and norms. They take pride in being above the law.

2. They are loyal only to themselves. They feel no guilt about using people and then abandoning them to move on.

3. They take pleasure in being shrewd and calculating.

4. They spot people's vulnerability and take them for all they are worth.

5. They become belligerent and vindictive if others cross them. They angrily deny any wrongdoing and always whip up a plausible explanation to take themselves off the hook.

6. They view openness and intimacy as signs of weakness—invitations to be exploited. Only weaklings have a conscience.

7. When things go their way, they are charming and friendly. But if their plans are frustrated, they become furious and combative. Their tempers can flare into verbal threats or physical violence since they have few internal restraints.

8. They believe that they will never be caught or punished.

9. They seek instant highs. That quest often leads them to alcohol and drugs, which they are convinced they can enjoy and control.

An antisocial counselee bragged to me about how he had used his older brother's credit card for more than five years, subtly billing hundreds of dollars of charges, but never enough at one time to attract his brother's attention. Finally, he charged three thousand dollars that his brother could never account for.

Con artists may put up a front of having a nice family life, yet behind the scenes terrify spouses and children. Or they may own a legitimate business and deal drugs on the side. One antisocial man managed a clothing store in the daytime and sexually molested little boys at night. Another man, a city councilman, owned a package liquor store, and he sold alcohol to minors for years.

BETWEEN MAN AND WOMAN

In man-woman relationships, con artists use the "bait and switch" routine. They make sweet promises before the marriage, but afterward they turn the tables. Dr. Jekyll changes into Mr. Hyde.

Harriet was a devout Christian woman who was naive about the darker side of human nature. Her first husband had left her for another woman a few years earlier, and she was eager to remarry. She answered an ad in the date section of a newspaper and met Jeff for coffee. He was tall and handsome, self-assured and charming. He took her to plays and dinner.

In answer to her questions about his past, he said he had just moved from another state because of a wonderful job offer. They were married, having known each other for two weeks. He moved into her home, and for three days, Harriet was ecstatically happy. Then she discovered that although Jeff said he was going to work every day, he didn't have a job. He charged thousands of dollars to her credit cards by the fourth week.

When she confronted Jeff, he became cold and furious. He threatened to leave her if she didn't withdraw her suspicions and avow her love. During the second month, Harriet found out that Jeff was seeing other women. She told him to leave, and she changed the locks on her doors to prevent his return. He responded by stalking her and shooting a rifle bullet through her front door. Harriet got a restraining order and moved secretly to a new location. A year later the police contacted her and said that Jeff had been arrested in another state for credit card fraud.

Con artists have a checkered history of relationships, including an on-again, off-again dating pattern and, most likely, several short-term marriages.

One woman embezzled thousands of dollars from a state-funded homeless shelter that she directed, knowing that her wealthy husband would have to pay it back if she was ever caught. She was caught. And he had to repay the money when she was sent to jail.

SEX IN MARRIAGE

Con artists don't like the feeling of being tied down in marriage, so they often develop a double life that lets them feel footloose and fancy-free. One married man bragged about seducing ten women in ten years without arousing his wife's suspicions. To him, that meant he was virile, irresistible, and clever.

In marriage, con artists are prone to pursue the darker side of sex—bondage, sadomasochism, pornography, and bizarre erotica. They may put pressure on their spouses to use alcohol or drugs in order to enhance sexual intensity. The hidden agenda is to make the wife or husband more spaced out and dependent by getting addicted to these substances.

Since con artists are truly callous and lack empathy for their partners, they demand what they want when they want it and then change the subject as soon as they are gratified.

When the antisocial partner meets another sexually desirable person, there is little in the way of conscience, duty, or loyalty to keep him or her from having an affair and lying if telltale signs are found.

THOUGHT PATTERN

The automatic self-talk of the con artist sounds like this:

- Deception gets you what you want.
- Survival of the fittest—the law of the jungle—is the best philosophy.
- Love is a joke. Self-sacrifice is ridiculous.
- Strike while the iron is hot. Take what you can get and run.
- It's a dog-eat-dog world.
- The world owes me a living.
- I get a thrill from breaking rules and thumbing my nose at authority.
- I'll always be independent and free.

EMOTIONAL LIFE

Con artists are thick-skinned and self-contained. They don't want to be emotionally connected to others because that could interfere with their freedom. They treat people like things to be manipulated.

A corporate executive named Dick made an appointment for him and his wife, Debbie, to see me for marriage counseling. When we met, he asked if he might speak to me for ten minutes before asking his wife to join us. I agreed.

Once inside my office, he looked me in the eye and said, "Dr. Montgomery, I've been having an affair with my secretary for six months. Now I want to marry her. I need you to help me get out of my current marriage. I'll pay you extra if you can arrange the counseling so that my wife ends up feeling guilty and responsible for our divorce. Then I can marry this other woman, and my wife will never know I had the affair."

I knew I had an antisocial personality on my hands.

"Dick, I appreciate you leveling with me at the beginning of counseling. But I may not be the counselor you're looking for. I won't enter a conspiracy with you against your wife. It is your decision to remain married or divorce, but it is my style to promote genuineness and honesty—not manipulation—in couple's counseling."

Dick thought for a moment. "Okay, I'll tell her about the affair if you can guarantee that she'll be okay and I can marry my secretary."

"I don't do deals," I said. "I invite you to tell your wife about the affair so that we can honestly hash out what's gone wrong over the years. Debbie needs to know where you're at so that she can make her own decisions. I suggest that we work for a couple of months on your relationship. If one of you concludes that the marriage is over, then we can move toward a sane and healthy parting of the ways."

After I brought Debbie in for the remainder of the session, Dick came clean about his affair. Debbie was shattered by the fact that he'd lied to her so convincingly for six months. He became caustic and furious, blaming her for making him fall in love with his secretary. He reacted as a con artist does when his scheming is exposed: blame others and excuse himself.

I wish I could say that Dick and Debbie recovered a happy marriage, but that did not happen. My main therapeutic focus over the next several months was preventing him from destroying her. The next session I saw Dick alone. He bragged about taking revenge on Debbie.

"I really messed up Debbie today," he said. "I hired a locksmith to change all the locks in our old house where she lives. I hired a towing company to tow her car away from work. I wish I could see the look on her face tonight!"

"Dick," I interrupted, "you're being cruel and aggressive. You're the one who had the affair and chose to leave her. I think you need to balance this out by being supportive. Get in touch with your caring if only for the well-being of your children. Debbie needs to establish a new life and to provide for them."

"But I hate her!" he raged.

Over the next few sessions, Dick saw that it was to his advantage to stop obstructing Debbie. Reluctantly, he quit harassing her and agreed to equitable child support. But, he reasoned, Debbie should have sex with him for being so nice. I explained to him that it didn't work that way.

Debbie was able to launch her single life with enough financial support and self-confidence to be successful. Dick married his secretary, and within three months he brought her in for counseling because of all the fights they were having.

Con artists experience no anxiety, guilt, or remorse about the impact of their choices on others. They are willing to go to any lengths to get what they want. Giving someone the shaft adds emotional excitement to the challenge.

PERCEPTION OF GOD

Con artists often avoid spirituality like the plague. It's as though they intuitively know that their evil and manipulative way of life is in direct opposition to the love of God. They try to avoid thinking about God unless they can use God's name to make money or seduce sexual partners Elmer Gantry style.

They think, *God prizes the strong and despises the weak. God created the laws of the jungle to reward the clever. God scorns the weak and uses them as cannon fodder for His grand designs. I am godlike and should use my powers for personal gain.*

The apostle Peter warns Christians about antisocial types who enter the ministry: "These teachers in their greed will tell you anything to get hold of your money. But God condemned them long ago and their destruction is on the way" (2 Peter 2:3 TLB).

In the Sermon on the Mount, Jesus warns, "Beware of false prophets, who come to you in sheep's clothing, but inwardly they are ravenous wolves" (Matt. 7:15).

For con artists who have a change of heart and decide to pursue a relationship with God, there remain strong temptations to pillage the coffers and fleece the sheep.

Cult leaders are often antisocial personalities. During the hostage standoff led by Branch Davidian minister David Koresh in Waco, Texas, I was interviewed and asked to describe Koresh's personality profile. I said that he was a mixture of paranoid and antisocial traits run amok. He was capable of a charismatic, but intimidating domination of his followers, he would be prone to sexually exploit women and girls, and if pushed into a corner, he could go out in a vindictive blaze of glory. That proved to be the case.

GROWTH AND CHANGE

Con artists sow the wind and reap the whirlwind. They lay the foundation for life and personality in sinking sand. Judas was an antisocial con artist—brash, rude, self-serving. He followed Christ but didn't surrender to a spiritual renewal. His antisocial pattern took over in the end. He betrayed his Master for thirty pieces of silver and then hanged himself. The Scripture is so true when it says, "But evil men and impostors will grow worse and worse, deceiving and being deceived" (2 Tim. 3:13).

Life isn't easy. No one owes us our dreams. Fulfillment comes from trusting in the Lord. Wrongdoing doesn't work. If con artists are willing to accept these truths, they begin to grow and change.

The first step of growth is to confess your sins and shortcomings to almighty God, asking Him to forgive you in the name of Jesus.

Accept God's forgiveness, and demonstrate your change of heart by making direct amends to everyone you have harmed. Receive the peace of Christ, and fellowship with others through the love the Holy Spirit gives you. Con artists are hard nuts to crack, and I've found that traditional psychotherapy seldom fazes them.

God's psychology calls for a spiritual birthing, followed by concrete steps to become a whole person. Jesus sets you free from antisocial trends, but you must keep resisting their temptation.

PRACTICAL GROWTH STRETCHES

1. As an antisocial type, you have to accept an unusual truth about yourself—you usually repress any sense of guilt or remorse. To find health and happiness, you need to learn the value of feeling guilty.

Healthy guilt alerts you to the fact that you have exploited someone to your advantage. It tells you that you have used another person as a thing and have dehumanized yourself in the process. This week try to become sensitive to the pangs of guilt when you are tempted to steal, lie, shirk responsibility, run up a credit card bill that you don't intend to pay, pull a shady business deal, or pull the wool over your spouse's eyes.

If you listen for the still, small voice of your spiritual conscience, the Holy Spirit will be able to communicate with you, showing you unhealthy behaviors and guiding you to healthy attitudes.

2. Commit yourself to several months of community service work. Serve in a soup kitchen, help out at the Salvation Army, or stop your car to pick up litter off the street. Acts of generosity and service counter your attitudes of thinking only about yourself and taking advantage of others.

When you catch yourself calculating and scheming about how to profit at someone's expense, stop. Pray for healing of your antisocial pattern. Ask the Lord to fill you with the Holy Spirit so that you can share in the humility and compassion of Jesus Christ.

3. Become willing to make amends to people you have harmed by your callous behavior. Join a twelve-step group to help you learn how to make a fearless moral inventory of your actions over the years. Learning to give up the exploitive approach to life will encourage you to share the pain and anxiety about relationships underlying your compulsion to use and abuse people.

Find a pastoral counselor to whom you can unburden yourself and confess your sins and shortcomings. There is no shortcut to developing your whole compass; you must face yourself honestly and disclose your hidden motives to God and to another person.

4. Read through this list of Scriptures to strengthen your conscience so that it can alert you to wrongdoing before the fact and help you to do the next right thing one day at a time.

So it was that when they gave God up and would not even acknowledge him, God gave them up to doing everything their evil minds could think of. Their lives became full of every kind of wickedness and sin, of greed and hate, envy, murder, fighting, lying, bitterness, and gossip. They were backbiters, haters of God, insolent, proud braggarts, always thinking of new ways of sinning. . . . They tried to misunderstand, broke their promises, and were heartless—without pity. They were fully aware of God's death penalty for these crimes, yet they went right ahead and did them anyway, and encouraged others to do them, too (Rom. 1:28–32 TLB).

These men mock and curse at anything they do not understand, and, like animals, they do whatever they feel like, thereby ruining their souls (Jude 10 TLB).

Those who trouble their households will inherit the wind (Prov. 11:29 NRSV).

The smooth tricks of evil men will be exposed, as will all the lies they use to oppress (Isa. 32:7 TLB).

Keep your tongue from evil,
And your lips from speaking deceit (Ps. 34:13).

Deceit is in the heart of those who devise evil,
But counselors of peace have joy. . . .
Lying lips are an abomination to the LORD,
But those who deal truthfully are His delight (Prov. 12:20–22).

5. In the past you have viewed openness and intimacy as signs of weakness and invitations for exploitation. This week seek a spirit of openness and intimacy in all of your interactions with people.

Speak to your spouse and a friend about your childhood and adolescent years, about how you learned to outsmart people instead of trusting them, and about how you learned the pattern of self-aggrandizement instead of cooperation and love. Ask these people to help you become aware of the antisocial trends listed in this chapter as you are manifesting them and to support your growth and change.

CHAPTER 7

Wallflowers

*Their frequent loneliness and sadness is maintained
by a fear of rejection, which inhibits the initiation or
deepening of friendships. . . . they may report that
they feel "like a robot" or are "going through life in a
dream."*

—Aaron Beck

Human beings have a deep, instinctive need to love and be loved. When abused or humiliated early in life, they conclude that something is wrong with them and that relationships bring only anguish.

People who function from the wallflower pattern don't feel invited to the party of life. They are bashful and avoidant. They retreat from the fellowship of humanity, although they may be quite gifted. The composer Tchaikovsky was a withdrawn wallflower. So was the philosopher Soren Kierkegaard, who wrote in his journal that he was "melancholy, soul-sick, profoundly and absolutely a failure in many ways."[1]

A SHADOW LIFE

A young woman named Diane came to me for counseling. She spoke so softly in our sessions that I could barely hear her. She loved children and animals but felt awkward around other adults. She was skittish and hypersensitive, a shy wallflower helplessly stuck on the weakness compass point.

Diane longed to be healed but greatly feared disclosing herself to me. She seemed to assume rejection. Early in counseling I identified the negative self-talk that automatically played in her mind. "I'm inadequate." "I'm ugly." "I don't have anything to offer." "If people really knew me, they'd reject me."

Where could such thoughts originate? After several weeks Diane whispered the shameful secret that had triggered her wallflower approach to life.

"When I was six, my uncle . . ."

I knew the rest. She didn't even have to finish the ugly story, which I'd heard all too often from other victims of sexual abuse. Diane's father abandoned the family when she was five. Her mother became withdrawn and helpless, modeling how to hide from life rather than deal with it. The vulnerable little girl became a prime target for her uncle, who molested her regularly until she was nine years old. Diane's shame kept her from telling anyone until the day she finally told me.

Even God, she felt, judged her as nasty and evil for letting such a terrible thing happen. Diane's life script came to be: "I am a bad person who deserves punishment. I deserve to be shamed and isolated."

I arranged for a psychiatrist to put Diane on antidepressant medication during the first year of counseling. The drug relieved her black moods. Such medication is sometimes advisable and even necessary for someone suffering major depression. After the fog of despair lifted, we more easily faced and resolved Diane's personality rigidities.

During the first few months of counseling, Diane brought me

journals filled with drawings that illustrated her inner agony and poor self-image. One drawing portrayed her identity confusion: two hands covering a face peekaboo style. Diane's painful helplessness was depicted in many pictures of women in various fetal positions. One poignant drawing captured her despair and hope for resurrection: a dead woman with an Easter lily growing out of her belly.

Our weekly sessions slowly awakened her instincts for self-preservation. Diane and I worked through the sexual abuse memories and nightmares until they stopped plaguing her.

I encouraged Diane to risk new behaviors that would serve as opportunities for growth. Before long she began to get her bearings, especially once she understood where she was located on the self compass. She learned to express herself calmly and clearly, to expand her artistic talents in commercial directions, and to develop personal identity and intimacy with others. Diane's intuitions and gut feelings grew more reliable. Her trust in the still, small voice of the Lord increased.

Whenever Diane demonstrated creative thinking, emotional expression, or assertive problem solving, I showered her with accolades. I cheered her on enthusiastically. Diane needed to know that she was not alone, that God and I were in her corner. I continued to praise her intelligence, sensitivity, and enterprising spirit until she internalized these positive evaluations of herself.

Diane showed promise as an artist. In the final phase of counseling, I coached her to set up a studio, negotiate professional fees, and deal with clients confidently. Suddenly, through an inspired period of creativity, a dozen color drawings poured out of her. These sensitive pieces included a fawn in the woods, a little girl playing with a butterfly, a group of swans swimming, an eagle in flight, and a child laughing.

I was especially touched by a rendition of baby Jesus being visited by a fawn, a mouse, a duck, a raccoon, and a butterfly. I felt that her new creativity was a gift of the Holy Spirit.

Now an accomplished wildlife artist and an author and illustrator of children's books, Diane speaks in high schools about abuse issues. She is a witness to the hope that with the grace of God's psychology, wallflowers can dislodge their rigid pattern and reveal their true potential in Christ.

WHAT MAKES WALLFLOWERS TICK?

Wallflowers are afraid of being hurt, rejected, and ridiculed. Their strategy is to back off or avoid getting involved in the first place. For avoidant wallflowers, here is a summary of the pattern:

1. They see themselves as socially inept and incompetent in academic or work situations. At work they avoid taking on new responsibilities or seeking advancement because they fear failure.

2. They don't initiate or deepen friendships. They distance from others to guard against the risk of hurt. They are so preoccupied with fears and insecurities that they constantly imagine they're in danger. They pursue the course of greatest safety, which is to take no risks at all.

3. In social situations they can experience palpitations, sweating, blushing, stomach cramps, and tension. They avoid direct eye contact. When feeling anxious, they "shut down" by standing in the corner or leaving at the first opportunity.

4. They draw a magic circle around themselves that no one can penetrate. Only in being alone do they gain a sense of relief. Theodore Millon writes, "These individuals maintain a constant vigil lest their impulses and longing for affection result in a repetition of the pain and anguish they have experienced with others previously. Only by active withdrawal can they protect themselves."[2]

5. They discount compliments by believing that people are putting them on. Their desires for affection are repressed, since attempts at bonding in the past have brought only pain.

6. They are compelled by inner fears to accommodate to mar-

ginal living conditions and tolerate bad relationships. They are afraid to change the status quo.

BETWEEN MAN AND WOMAN

Avoidant spouses distrust the mate's genuine caring, and they constantly fear rejection. They feel lucky to have landed a marriage partner at all. They are inwardly convinced that the other person will find them inadequate before long. Because they are on the lookout for the least sign of derision, they impose a strain on the spouse. Because wallflowers are hesitant to trust or confide anything about the inner life, the spouse has difficulty consummating the marriage emotionally, intellectually, or sexually.

A wallflower may exasperate the spouse by constant aversive testing, saying things like the following:

- "I'm sorry I can't do anything right."
- "Now you know what a klutz I am."
- "What do you possibly see in me?"
- "Aren't you sorry you married me?"

At first these statements draw sympathy from the partner, but after months and years of trying to talk the wallflower out of the negative assumptions, the partner may either reject the wallflower or simply give up.

When the spouse questions them about why they refuse to cope, or when the spouse shows exasperation about their perpetual helplessness, they take it as confirmation that they are failures and lapse deeper into depression as a way of avoiding once again. On more hopeful days, they begin a new cycle of good intentions by saying, "One day I'll wake up and everything will be fine."

SEX IN MARRIAGE

Wallflowers are generally terrified of sex. They are unwilling to take emotional and interpersonal risks, period. Sex is the greatest risk of all, requiring the greatest psychological nakedness and the most spiritual openness.

Wallflowers are convinced that they are physically unattractive and sexually inadequate. They expect to be used sexually and eventually humiliated and rejected. Their negative anticipation makes these self-fulfilling prophecies come true. At the slightest hint from a spouse that they are not perfect, they'll withdraw into a cavern of depression, sometimes assuming a fetal position for hours. Once curled up in the safe womb of despair, they are reluctant to venture out again.

Wallflowers are split off from their bodies and can regard marital sex with disdain. Avoidant men tend to be unimaginative, repetitive, and inexpressive in sex. Many avoidant women are willing to live without sex or to become passive bodies for the partner's sexual release.

One avoidant woman told me that her husband had humiliated her seventeen years ago on their wedding night, and that she'd never felt comfortable with sex again. I asked her what he did. She blushed, stammered, and said, "He made a horrible comment right after our first intercourse."

"What did he say?" I asked.

"He said, 'That was great sex!'" she replied.

"What was so offensive about that?" I asked.

"He must have been making fun of me. I didn't know anything about sex. How could it have been great?"

"Did you ever mention your negative assumption to him to find out what he really meant?"

"Of course not," she said, "I just withdrew from sex for seventeen years."

THOUGHT PATTERN

The automatic self-talk of avoidant wallflowers goes like this:

- I'd like to be accepted, but I know that people are out to degrade me.

- No matter how hard I try, nothing works out—I may as well give up.
- Dreams and fantasy are better than reality.
- No one is as scared and embarrassed as I am.
- If my parents don't like me, how could anyone?
- I need to maintain privacy and distance.
- If others really knew me, they'd reject me.
- No risk is worth taking.
- I must guard against disappointment at all costs.

Ironically, despite their hypersensitivity to painful feelings, wallflowers shy away from identifying unpleasant thoughts. They are unwilling to face or discuss their negative thought patterns.

EMOTIONAL LIFE

The main emotions of wallflowers are a combination of anxiety and sadness. Since they are introspective and monitor feelings continually, they are acutely aware of these painful feelings. Feelings of loneliness and of being unwanted are common. Because their emotions are so blocked, they may accumulate an inner world rich in fantasy and imagination. Their need for self-expression may be redirected into music, poetry, and soul-searching diaries that no one will ever read.

> *Wallflowers may accumulate an inner world rich in fantasy and imagination.*

To most people, wallflowers appear to be timorous or perhaps cold. But those who know them better recognize their sensitivity.

Wallflowers long for love but are convinced that people don't like them. They hope for grace but feel guilty. They pine for friendship but feel estranged. They may seek to avoid unpleasant feelings by using food, cigarettes, or alcohol to numb themselves.

Psychiatrist Paul Tournier writes, "Shyness, feelings of inferiority, lack of self-confidence, hypersensitivity, pathological feelings of guilt, emotional instability, panic, and indecision . . . maintain in the subject a feeling of weakness which provokes him to further weak reactions."[3]

Wallflowers usually have no close friends or confidants. The only companion may be a pet cat or dog who will not reject them.

PERCEPTION OF GOD

Avoidant wallflowers are nervous about a one-to-one encounter with God. "God doesn't really like or love me," they believe. "He hates misfits who are as unattractive, socially awkward, and boring as I am. God wants me to suffer. He requires penance for all the things I've done wrong. I always feel guilty about God, so I try not to get His attention."

Their gray-colored glasses make them see God as disinterested and rejecting of them. But when they take these depressing lenses off, they can see Him as helpful, supportive, and interested in them. Listen to Christ's words in the Sermon on the Mount:

> Blessed are the poor in spirit,
>   For theirs is the kingdom of heaven.
> Blessed are those who mourn,
>   For they shall be comforted.
> Blessed are the meek,
>   For they shall inherit the earth (Matt. 5:3–5).

Their weakness gives them special access to the resourcefulness of God and the comfort of the Holy Spirit. If wallflowers offer Him their weakness, God can help them find the beauty in the stone.

GROWTH AND CHANGE

If you are stuck in the avoidant personality pattern, the first thing is facing it without feeling crushed. It is a fact of life that you can accept and change. The second thing is realizing that you can remain avoidant as long as you wish. The third thing is becoming willing to take off your gray-colored glasses. I know about wallflowers—I spent a few years as one.

I tried out the bully and prima donna roles in high school, but as a freshman in college, I felt very reserved around people. I had deep-seated fears that others didn't like me. At social gatherings, I always arrived late and left early. I was terrified to raise my hand in classes because my face would turn a brilliant red and my armpits would perspire like crazy. Even worse, my voice would sound hollow and far away, and I'd forget what I was going to say next.

If a group of people were talking among themselves, I'd assume that they were saying something bad about me or that they'd resent it if I joined them. If several students went for lunch, I wouldn't dare tag along.

I remember really praying about this: "God, why do I feel so different from everybody else? Why am I so sensitive to the least signs of rejection? Why am I so self-conscious all the time?"

I sought out a college counselor. With stammering lips, I explained my problems. He arranged for me to join a therapy group in progress.

One day in group therapy, the therapist said that many people live with a needless fear of others. He said that this fear could be transformed into a new level of comfort and confidence. I didn't know it then, but he was saying that wallflowers can discover their strength and assertion compass points, and develop personality wholeness. Scared to death, I raised my hand and admitted that I was afraid of people.

"Would you like to try an experiment, Dan?" the therapist asked.

I felt so vulnerable in front of everybody. But I knew that I had to make a breakthrough. I had to lower the drawbridge and come out of my lonely castle. It seemed to be the time.

"Yes," I said, my palms sweating profusely.

The therapist invited five other students to form an impromptu group and start talking among themselves. They warmed up to each other quickly and really got into it. Then he asked me to stand up and approach the group.

I stood up, but I couldn't take another step.

The therapist asked the group to freeze the action. They did, standing there motionless like I was. Then he asked me what automatic thoughts I was thinking.

"What self-talk is going through your head right now, Dan?"

"They look like they're doing fine without me," I said. "I don't have anything to say. They're bound to reject me."

The therapist asked me to walk among the five people while they were still frozen and look at each one up close. I did so.

"Dan, what are you noticing?" he asked.

"Well—they look like normal people. They look friendly enough. They look like they're just talking to one another."

"Congratulations, Dan. You just took off your gray-colored glasses. You're seeing them as normal human beings who'd be as interested in you as they are in each other. Now I'm going to unfreeze them. I want you to join in with them."

I suddenly realized that my fantasy of rejection was a distortion in my mind. It was something *I* could change whenever I decided.

I joined the group, waited for a break in the conversation, and then introduced myself. Within a few minutes I was talking as comfortably as anybody else. The therapist called a halt to the experiment.

When we all sat down, he asked the group members how they perceived me. They shared comments like: "Dan seems like an interesting person"; "He seems shy, but he's got a lot to say once he opens up." One girl giggled and said, "I wish he'd ask me for a date!"

That day was a milestone in my development. I had walked out of my cavern of depression, and I felt exhilarated. I knew that I'd still wear my gray-colored glasses from time to time. But I could recognize them and take them off more frequently.

Wallflowers benefit from God's psychology by reminding themselves daily that they are unique in His eyes. Strength and confidence will come as they actively pursue God's will. Obstacles become challenges. Challenges become adventures in personal growth. They forget to depress themselves because they finally feel alive and involved. They take on more responsibility at home and at work. Humor, poise, and confidence begin shining through. The beauty in the stone is released.

PRACTICAL GROWTH STRETCHES

1. Make a conscious decision to outgrow the avoidant wallflower pattern. Pray for the Holy Spirit's daily assistance in rooting out negative self-talk. Instead of thinking, _I'm stupid,_ think, _I'm as intelligent as the next person._ Instead of thinking, _I'm unattractive,_ think, _I have my own unique looks and can improve them if I wish._

Believe that God specializes in loving people like you. Throw your negative self-talk into the garbage pail as quickly as you become aware of it. Make a choice for positive self-talk instead.

2. Decide to actively develop your skills, talents, and potentials. Quit making excuses for how hard life is or how futile it is to try anything. What are your gifts and talents? Find a mentor or pay someone to help you develop your strengths.

Active self-development is the opposite of avoidant withdrawal. If

> _Quit making excuses for how hard life is or how futile it is to try anything._

you're athletic, get a coach to work with you. If you're intellectual, sign up for college courses. If you're artistic, hire a tutor. If you need help with finances, child care, or housing, seek out a community agency. Honor whatever cries out for expression within you. Lay aside your fears and get on with life.

3. If you still feel haunted or traumatized by painful events in your past, make an appointment with a therapeutic counselor. Face and work through psychological blocks from the past so you can live effectively in the present.

If need be, join a twelve-step group to receive immediate help and fellowship in your area of need—for instance, if you have an eating disorder, join Overeaters Anonymous, or if you were abused as a child, join a Children of Adult Alcoholics or Incest Survivors group. God will meet you within these groups and heal you as you work the twelve steps. Another alternative is to start a self compass group in your church following the guidelines presented at the end of this book.

4. Meditate on the following Scriptures, asking God to quicken them in your heart and mind. Call upon these verses when you need help.

> The LORD is my light and my salvation;
> Whom shall I fear?
> The LORD is the strength of my life;
> Of whom shall I be afraid? (Ps. 27:1).

> Peace I leave with you, My peace I give to you; not as the world gives do I give to you. Let not your heart be troubled, neither let it be afraid (John 14:27).

> And we know that all things work together for good to those who love God, to those who are the called according to His purpose (Rom. 8:28).

> For I am persuaded that neither death nor life, nor angels nor principalities nor powers, nor things present nor things to come,

nor height nor depth, nor any other created thing, shall be able to separate us from the love of God which is in Christ Jesus our Lord (Rom. 8:38–39).

My God shall supply all your need according to His riches in glory by Christ Jesus (Phil. 4:19).

For God has not given us a spirit of fear, but of power and of love and of a sound mind (2 Tim. 1:7).

There is no fear in love; but perfect love casts out fear (1 John 4:18).

Don't you know by now that the everlasting God, the Creator of the farthest parts of the earth, never grows faint or weary? . . . They that wait upon the Lord shall renew their strength. They shall mount up with wings like eagles; they shall run and not be weary; they shall walk and not faint (Isa. 40:28, 31 TLB).

Now to Him who is able to keep you from stumbling,
And to present you faultless
Before the presence of His glory with exceeding joy,
To God our Savior, . . .
Be glory and majesty,
Dominion and power,
Both now and forever.
Amen (Jude 24–25).

5. Quit being overprotective about your fragile ego. Taking a few risks is better than sitting out the game of life on the bench. Praise yourself for your tiniest successes. Catch God blessing you and thank Him daily.

This week dare to walk up to a group of people and join them. As you persist in this exercise, your former irrational fears will leave. You'll eventually feel a tangible peace around other people.

CHAPTER 8

Hermits

Individuals with this disorder . . . may seem vague about their goals, indecisive in their actions, self-absorbed, absentminded, and detached from their environment ("not with it" or "in a fog").

—American Psychiatric Association

I snuggled up in his arms in the maple rocking chair, tucked cozily with a warm blanket on a cold New Mexico night. My fever had broken from the croup. My daddy's love cradled me tenderly.

I was five years old. It was the last time he hugged me for twenty-five years.

The men at Phillips Petroleum Company called my father Shotgun because of his hair-trigger temper. Once Phillips gave him a cheap alarm clock for winning a sales contest. He hurled it into the Rio Grande River. Being a very adventurous kid, I often found myself on the other end of Daddy's belt.

As a salesman, Dad would leave home Monday morning and return Friday night. The scratching sound of his key in the front door would bring me scurrying down the hall to get my "sackie." He'd take off his gray hat and hand me the brown paper bag. I'd thrust in my fingers and out would come a shiny red top, a bag full of cat's-eye marbles, or a boxcar for my train set. I longed for Dad to stay and play, but he would head straight to his den and close the door.

Exhausted from the week, Dad would spend the weekend doing what he really wanted to do—still life photography in his den. When he was home, the door was always closed. During the week when Dad was out of town, I'd tiptoe in as though to sense his presence in the room.

Birds—sparrows, grackles, robins—flocked to the feeding tray in Dad's den window year-round. Daddy loved those birds. Daddy loved a lot of things: dinosaurs, mystery novels, trout fishing. Sometimes I wondered if Daddy loved me.

When I was seven, I asked Dad to take me to a Jerry Lewis movie. He frowned, but he took me. I howled and shook with laughter until I noticed that he was sitting stone faced. When we left, he said, "That wasn't so funny." I seldom belly laughed again.

Whenever I would tag along with Dad to weddings or funerals, I'd notice that he never smiled or talked to anyone. We would arrive late and leave early. Slowly, these patterns crept into my life. I became shy around people and tongue-tied about feelings.

On my tenth birthday, Dad pulled something out of his pocket at the dinner table and said, "Here." He handed me a little tin box with five hand-tied trout flies in it—a Rio Grande King, a Royal Coachman, a Silver Doctor, an Irresistible, and a March Brown. I placed the box in the top of my chest of drawers. I never used those flies. They were too beautiful. They were proof of Daddy's love.

By eleven years old, though, my doubts were growing. It seemed like Dad was avoiding me. When he took me to get a haircut, he never said a word and always walked a good five steps in front of me. Did that mean he didn't like me?

"Charles, take Danny fishing this weekend," I can hear my mom saying. Or, "Charles, why don't you play catch with your son?"

Dad would let the steam build up in his pressure cooker and then explode. "Okay, Anna Mae! Now shut up!"

One summer morning Mom harangued him into taking me on a 120-mile business trip to Santa Rosa. Embarrassed, I ran upstairs to my room. I didn't like her forcing me on Dad. A few minutes later there was a knock on my door. "Danny, get ready to go to Santa Rosa," he said in a monotone.

That trip turned into one endless, lonely day. I waited for him to speak, but he never did. I dogged his footsteps around Santa Rosa as he made business calls. I numbed myself to block out the painful sense of feeling unwanted. We were together six hours. Not one word passed between us.

One night when I'd entered puberty, I ventured into his den longing for understanding about my budding masculinity. Dad stopped typing and looked up from his report.

"Whatcha want?"

Heat rushed to my face. "Daddy, what do you do when your body does things you don't want it to, and you think about girls all day?" I blurted out.

He looked at me with a poker face. "Self-control," he said, turning back to his typewriter.

The silence between us grew into a sprawling chasm during my teenage years. In college I tried twice to talk to Dad about the meaning of life. He didn't like eye contact, and his mind was made up on all subjects. Once I asked him about his own childhood. All he said was, "I lost my parents when I was six. My aunt raised me."

When I entered medical school after college, Dad seemed proud of me. But I was having second thoughts. I began to feel that my true calling lay in the ministry.

I drove back to my hometown for Thanksgiving and knocked on Dad's den door.

"What is it?" he asked.

"Dad, do you think God talks to people?"

"No," he replied.

"But I keep getting the strange feeling that God is leading me away from medical school, maybe to seminary."

"That's crazy. You need a job with security and a retirement program." As so often before, he turned back to the typewriter.

I pressed one step further. "Daddy, God is calling me to follow Him, and I'm going to go."

Shotgun stood up and confronted me with a furious glare. I had always longed for him to look me in the eyes but never like this. "If you leave medical school, it will be the worst mistake of your life," he said.

I ran into the living room, grabbed the suitcase I had just set down, and endured a long midnight drive back to school. I spent Thanksgiving alone.

I resigned from medical school several weeks later. I spent the next three years in seminary, and then finished a Ph.D. in counseling psychology at the University of New Mexico. I was twenty-nine. Dad remained curt and distant the whole time. When he said anything at all, it was that psychology was the most worthless profession on earth, aside from theology.

I took a job as a college professor and wrote my first book integrating Christianity and psychology. When I received the first copy in the mail, I autographed it for Dad. As soon as I could, I flew home to visit my folks. My heart speeded up as I pictured presenting Dad with the signed copy of the book. I found him sitting in the maple rocking chair next to the fireplace, reading a book about dinosaurs.

I walked over and stood in front of him with my new book in my hands. I wanted to give him a sackie. The little boy in me wanted to jump up and down and shout, "I did it, Daddy! I wrote a book about God and families! Thousands of people have bought it, and here is your own special copy!" But I just stood there mute.

*I learned just in time
that the best way to
find love is to express
love, that God will
help us overcome
fear, and that the
wisest time to say,
"I love you," is
right now.*

He glanced up from his book. "Whatcha got?"

I handed him the book. He looked at the cover. I held my breath. "That's nice," he said as he put the book on the floor. He resumed reading about dinosaurs. Daddy never mentioned the book again.

Stunned, I retreated to my room. Then I went out and got drunk. I sat in a back booth of a bar, tears streaming down my cheeks. "Dear God," I sobbed, "am I ever going to feel accepted? Is there anything I can do to get Dad's love?"

I got no answer that night. But over the next few months I had a series of four dreams.

In the first dream, I was talking to Dad long-distance. He responded with the usual three-word replies. I got a fantastic urge to tell him that I loved him. The intense emotion startled me out of slumber. "Am I the one, Lord," I asked, "who has to *overcome my own reserve* and reach out *first?*"

In the next dream, Dad and I were talking on the phone again. I decided that he was never going to use the *l*-word. I took the risk and blurted out, "I love you, Dad." He hung up on me.

In the third dream, I told him over the phone that he had been a good father in many ways. I said that I wanted us to be friends. He said, "How?"

In the fourth dream, I was carrying my suitcase up to my parents' front porch for a Christmas visit. Dad stood on the porch. I hugged him. I awoke from the dream in a sweat.

Christmas vacation arrived. I took a bus from the Albuquerque airport to my hometown where a taxi delivered me to my parents' door. A voice inside seemed to whisper, *Now is the time.*

I stamped the snow off my shoes on the front porch and knocked on the door. Dad opened it. I stepped across the threshold and clasped him in an awkward embrace. His body froze, but he mumbled, "Welcome home, son." He had never welcomed me home before.

Over the holidays I asked him about his recent cancer treatments. "I'm scared, Danny," he said. "Twice a week they put me into a big contraption with a narrow tunnel. I get claustrophobic and think I'll go nuts."

A feeling! Dad had shared an emotion with me. Wow! At one point I looked up to find his eyes on mine. He quickly looked away.

Sunday morning I had to pack for the return flight. In the top drawer of my old chest, my fingers touched something in the right back corner. I pulled out a little tin case. Inside were five hand-tied trout flies, perfectly preserved.

After breakfast, Mom and Dad accompanied me to the door. The taxi waited outside, steam oozing out the tailpipe.

I stepped into the cold and paused. That old paralysis of emotional numbness gripped me. Then the dreams flashed through my consciousness.

I grabbed my father in a full-bodied bear hug. "Daddy, I love you!" I said into his ear.

His arms moved slowly to my shoulders. He cradled me gently and whispered, "I love you, too, Danny."

Daddy died three weeks later.

At his funeral a joy consoled the sadness within me. I hoped that Shotgun was now being rocked in the arms of his heavenly Father, just as he had rocked me long ago.

I learned just in time that the best way to find love is to express love, that God will help us overcome our fear, and that the wisest time to say, "I love you," is right now. These are lessons that schizoid hermits need to learn.

WHAT MAKES HERMITS TICK?

The term *schizoid* is composed of the prefix *schizo-*, from the Greek word meaning "split," and the suffix *oid*, which means "like." Schizoid hermits are split off from their own feelings and insensitive to the emotions of others. They live in a world of their own. Psychologist Rollo May called schizoids "hollow people," and he wrote that "hollow people do not have a base from which to learn to love."[1]

Schizoid hermits can be creative in occupations that allow for solitary work. But any required contact with people makes them ill at ease. They may pursue reclusive hobbies outside the work environment, and they are standoffish with the spouse and children.

The schizoid and avoidant personalities are stuck on the weakness compass point, tending to feel like misfits who can't make it in society. Both are likely to be socially hesitant and reserved. But where the avoidant wallflower still longs to be socially accepted and is painfully aware of rejection, the schizoid hermit is socially indifferent and has no desire for meaningful interaction.

Hermits seek to solve the problem of interpersonal anxiety in an ingenious way—through not caring about people any longer. They share these characteristics:

1. They regard human relationships as messy, problematic, and undesirable.

2. They consider themselves to be observers rather than participants in society. They are self-sufficient loners.

3. They are indifferent to people's praise or criticism. They don't care what others think of them.

4. They have no motivation to acquire social graces or social interests.

5. They are easily overwhelmed with social communication at work or at home. If a situation demands too much from them, they panic and beat a hasty exit.

6. They want to pursue their hobbies without any intrusions on their time or energy.

7. They are sometimes aware that life seems bland, empty, and unfulfilling, and they accept that with apathetic resignation.

8. They can develop patterns of ignoring family members, which makes them emotionally absent spouses and parents.

9. Their goals are negative: not to be involved, not to need anyone, not to allow others to influence them or get close to them.

Laurel worked for an engineering firm. She experienced a crisis when her company wanted to promote her to a higher paying job that involved slightly more contact with colleagues. She had sequestered herself for ten years in a little office at the far end of a hallway where she could keep her door closed and attend to business with no social interaction. She was having anxiety attacks at night as she fretted about talking to people in her new position.

Fortunately for Laurel, she became aware of her schizoid pattern in time to challenge it. She turned the promotion into an opportunity for personality growth. By the time six months had passed in the new job, she had made considerable progress in her communication skills and social graces.

BETWEEN MAN AND WOMAN

Hermits fall into relationships while still feeling ambivalent. They may date or marry, but it's usually because of pressure from the family, or they may experience a fleeting fancy for a mate.

How does a schizoid person attract a partner to begin with? Usually, another person feels a need to rescue the hermit from a dreary life. Recognizing that the hermit lives in a bleak and unemotional world, a potential partner hopes to save, inspire, and help the hermit. But without the hermit's active desire and request for help, the venture is doomed to failure.

Some partners are impressed with what they believe to be the hermit's hidden brilliance. As one woman said, "He doesn't ever say anything. That means he's very deep." Wrong. It means that his thought processes are as barren as the Mojave Desert.

A woman may be vulnerable to falling for the strong, silent type of man; she thinks he understands the mysteries of life and will protect and love her. But if the man is a hermit, a severe disappointment is around the corner for her. He won't tell her how he feels because he doesn't know. He won't ask how she feels because he doesn't care. He won't talk to her most of the time because he wants to be left alone. And when he does talk, his thoughts seem disjointed and obscure because they are.

Hermits are not gentle or affectionate. They can say hello to you one day and totally ignore you the next. They can live in a house with you without saying a word. They are emotionally flat during holidays, celebrations, and memorable moments. They can ruin festive occasions by responding like mummies. Schizoid hermits view emotional needs or expressions from spouses as immature and distasteful. They don't want any emotional involvement with the family, preferring to live and let live. They let family matters ride along without direction or communication. They don't want to be bothered. Spouses feel frustrated when they realize that hermits have a distinct inability to carry on conversations and only grudgingly participate in life.

It's common for hermits to claim one room of the house—my dad chose his den; a woman might choose her workshop or sewing room—as a private sanctuary in which they live undisturbed. Regular withdrawal into that sanctuary appears to family members as a sign of rejection but actually represents their disinterest in relating.

SEX IN MARRIAGE

Hermits report little or no desire for sexual experiences. One reason is that they are split off from their bodies as much as their emotions. Their bodies are too numb to enjoy the pleasure of sexual stimulation. They are too emotionally shut down to experience the joy of sensuality. The fact that sexual intercourse involves another person is a turnoff in itself. They would prefer solitary masturbation or a celibate life even though married.

Because they seek a sexual release only when the biological need forces itself, they are oblivious to a spouse's invitations, cues, or direct suggestions for lovemaking. Hermits don't view sexual intercourse as lovemaking. Sex is more of a mechanical chore to be performed when biological pressure demands it. They like to get it over with as quickly as possible.

Hermits offer no verbal intimacy, no cuddling, no warm afterglow. They don't notice how attractive spouses look or how sexy spouses try to be. They refuse to talk about how to make sex more enjoyable or interesting. Spouses of hermits usually report that their sex lives are empty, unimaginative, and joyless.

THOUGHT PATTERN

The automatic self-talk of the schizoid hermit goes like this:

- I prefer to be alone.
- Emotional relationships are entanglements that I don't need.
- My motto is "live and let live."
- When people are out of sight, they are out of mind.
- I stay safe by keeping an invisible, impenetrable circle around me.
- I sometimes feel empty and depressed with my humdrum life.
- I feel lethargic and fatigued much of the time.
- Sometimes life seems barren and meaningless.

EMOTIONAL LIFE

Events that provoke joy, anger, or sadness in others produce no response in hermits. Emotions are blunted no matter what their nature, positive or negative.

A friend can marry, but they'll feel no excitement. A parent can die, and they'll mention it in a matter-of-fact monotone. A child

> *Events that pro-voke joy, anger, or sadness in others produce no response in hermits.*

can graduate, and they may not even show up. They like being aloof.

Hermits actively avoid interpersonal events like the birth of a child, children's school events, and the social activities of their spouses. A son told me in tears that he had been an all-state wrestler in high school. His schizoid father never attended a single match. A woman shared her shock and sorrow with me that her husband didn't come to the hospital for her labor and childbirth. He said he was busy tinkering in the garage.

Another woman was with her six-week-old infant in the emergency room. She had just revived him from a SIDS (sudden infant death syndrome) episode. Her husband was informed but never showed up. He said it was just too much for him.

PERCEPTION OF GOD

The schizoid pattern presents a formidable barrier to a relationship with God. Hermits view God as detached, impersonal, and uninvolved. The prospect of being touched by His love is disconcerting.

The hermit thinks, *God is like a hermit. He doesn't care about people. God put the universe in motion but leaves people to fend for themselves. He doesn't answer prayers because He doesn't care what happens. God is oblivious to human needs and feelings.*

Hermits try to avoid church, Bible studies, and prayer groups. But when they do attend, they make only marginal commitments.

At best they tend to avoid God and people, yet they may want to research abstract theological arguments or read about bizarre doctrinal spin-offs.

GROWTH AND CHANGE

Hermits may lack the inner desire to become active agents in living, choosing, and caring.

Warren was catapulted into looking at himself because his wife of fifteen years told him she needed a six-month separation. This distinguished-looking man with a shock of white hair came face-to-face with his lonely life. He told me that he loved his wife, Shelley, and wanted to make a go of it.

I recognized his schizoid pattern in our first session. Right away I noticed his limp handshake. He avoided eye contact, absently flipped his fingers through his hair, and spoke in a disjointed monotone. His body was heavily armored with muscular tension, his chest barely moving when he breathed.

During the first month of counseling, Warren couldn't seem to grasp what I was suggesting, that he was the cause of his empty life. I kept searching for some sort of emotional trauma in childhood that might account for his withdrawal. Finally, I found it in his relationship with his mother.

Warren's mother totally invaded his personality and spoiled him rotten. She was an arrogant woman who smothered him with too much attention. She never let him develop an identity apart from her.

"I still remember Mom making me wear an angora bonnet to my first day of kindergarten," he said with gritted teeth. "I felt so helpless."

"Can we pray together for God to stir up your old memories so that we can get them out of your system?" I asked.

"But I don't want to have feelings," he said. "They're too painful."

"That's only because you were never allowed to express them. They got all bunched up inside, and you built a wall of armor to keep them there. But that wall has kept you from being open and loving with your wife and kids."

Something cracked him open as I spoke, and some of the armor began to fall away. God was already answering his needs. He sobbed and said that he felt sorry for all the missed opportunities for intimacy. "I recognize that I've been a fool," he said, "and that I've been the one who has made our marriage a quiet hell."

> *God's psychology requires that hermits reconnect with the world and learn to shape it with courage and love.*

Over the next several weeks, he recovered many childhood and adolescent memories along with the emotions that accompanied them. One by one, we processed his long-buried feelings of humiliation, anger, sadness, and anxiety. Each week his face grew more animated and his voice increased in resonance. His breathing deepened and his body relaxed.

By the sixth month of counseling, in a session with Shelley, Warren ably expressed his deep regrets and committed himself to show his love to her without reservation. We still had to work on ways for him to do that, but the deepest impasse was bridged. He was exchanging his hermit existence for a more colorful life of trust, affection, and self-identity.

Warren and I are examples of many people with schizoid trends who reawaken long-buried emotions, give up reserve, and reach out to others with growing confidence. The wisdom of God's psychology requires that we reconnect with the world and learn to shape it with courage and love.

PRACTICAL GROWTH STRETCHES

1. As a hermit, you're going to have to muster considerable courage if you want to have a better life. The whole defense system that you have constructed against relating to others has to be

dismantled, one brick at a time. You've got to face your anxiety and lack of social skills.

Set aside an entire month to practice talking to people. Talk to waiters in a restaurant, clerks in a store, the mail carrier, the service station attendant, and people at the spa. Talk to your spouse and kids. Talk to your parents or write them a letter. It doesn't matter what you say. Just open your mouth and talk. You are now making real contact with other human beings, and this is the first step toward having a whole personality.

2. Give up the illusion that you can make it through life alone. It is a miserable way to live, devoid of friendship, compassion, and burden sharing. Your splendid isolation is really a crucifixion of your soul.

Make amends to others for being an emotionally absent spouse, parent, or worker. Just say, "I realize that I have a longtime pattern of not caring about people and not responding to feelings. I'm sorry for being this way around you, and I would like you to help me to change." You cannot change by an act of will; you need the help and support of others to whom you are reaching out.

3. Give up your cynicism about relationships and emotions. Make up five new thoughts this week to affirm that people are valuable and emotions are important. Here is an example: "I really care about the emotional well-being of people in my family"; or "It is important to know how to express love and anger, sadness and joy." Repeat this positive self-talk in your head every time your old cynical thoughts surface.

4. Ask the Holy Spirit to vitalize your soul and stir your heartfelt potential for life and relationships. Contemplate the following Scriptures, asking God to help you find beauty in your personality.

> O dry bones, hear the word of the LORD! . . . "Surely I will cause breath to enter into you, and you shall live. . . . Then you shall know that I am the LORD" (Ezek. 37:4–6).

You are like whitewashed tombs, which on the outside look beautiful, but inside they are full of the bones of the dead (Matt. 23:27 NRSV).

He who comes to God must believe that He is, and that He is a rewarder of those who diligently seek Him (Heb. 11:6).

Oh, taste and see that the LORD is good;
happy are those who take refuge in him (Ps. 34:8 NRSV).

I will give them one heart, and I will put a new spirit within them, and take the stony heart out of their flesh, and give them a heart of flesh . . . and they shall be My people, and I will be their God (Ezek. 11:19–20).

It is written:
"Eye has not seen, nor ear heard,
Nor have entered into the heart of man
The things which God has prepared for those who love Him"
(1 Cor. 2:9).

5. Act on your positive self-talk by daring to tell other people how you are feeling. The diplomatic sharing of emotions is the better part of intimacy and love, but it can take practice to master. You must start with baby steps, such as saying to yourself how you are feeling.

A feeling can be defined as the most private, emotionally colored part of your perception. You can usually tell a feeling because it's the hardest thing to share. You feel vulnerable and open to rejection. But share feelings you must if you are to be a whole person.

CHAPTER 9

Big Shots

These individuals overvalue their personal worth, direct their affections towards themselves rather than others, and expect that others will recognize their unique and special value.

—Theodore Millon and George S. Everly, Jr.

Kathy, an experienced professor of English, began teaching at a new college in a city where she had recently moved. She was expected to work closely with two colleagues, Emily and Peggy, who had established the department.

Kathy had no difficulty jumping into her new responsibilities. Beaming with confidence, she zeroed in on her classroom lectures and spoke out at staff meetings. During departmental meetings, she informed Emily and Peggy about the best way to teach English.

But one day halfway through the semester, her colleagues called a special meeting. Emily and Peggy were already sitting at the conference table when Kathy arrived. She noticed that they didn't smile as she sat down, even though she did.

"Kathy," said Emily, "Peggy and I need to talk with you about your behavior since you've been working here."

Kathy's chin lifted. "Oh?" she asked, eyeing Emily and Peggy.

"Yes," said Emily. "Peggy and I explained when you started here that we work as a team in this department. Decisions are made jointly by all of us. But we find that you are so self-absorbed that it's impossible for us to work with you."

"Yes," agreed Peggy. "Most of our meetings are spent on how well your classes are going and how creative your ideas are. I wonder if you care how our input might improve your teaching?"

Kathy glared at Peggy for a moment, then lowered her eyes. "No one has ever told me anything like this before," she said slowly.

Emily added, "We've worked too hard in establishing a quality program to have it obliterated by someone who's only out for herself. The last straw for me came last week when you informed our academic dean that the English department had offered you a new course on Chaucer—you hadn't even discussed it with us!"

Kathy cleared her throat. "I guess I've got some learning to do."

In a calm and straightforward way, without argument or rancor, the two women gave Kathy the feedback they thought she needed. Kathy learned that the English department was not going to center on her, and that she couldn't call all the shots. Narcissistic big shots can expand their self compasses when their need for admiration is frustrated and their ploys for special attention are no longer honored.

WHAT MAKES BIG SHOTS TICK?

The term *narcissism* comes from the classical Greek myth about Narcissus, a young man who fell in love with his image in the reflection of a pool. Like Narcissus, big shot personalities feel superior to others and entitled to royal treatment. They have an overbearing self-confidence, believing themselves to be extraordinary, whether or not that is actually true. They come to believe the myth of personal greatness. They automatically expect admiration because they adore themselves.

Big shots are stuck on the strength compass point. Their behavior is characterized by claiming center stage, preening, and flaunting. They actively resist the weakness and love points of their personalities, preferring to appear strong and exceptional. They lack the humility that comes from the weakness point, and the appreciation of others that comes from the love point. They use the assertion point occasionally, mainly to disparage or dismiss people who are not enthralled by them.

The narcissistic personality pattern shares with the histrionic pattern a need for admiration. But while prima donnas actively solicit attention from others, big shots disdain dependency. Big shots use a nonchalant, coolly superior style for gaining admiration.

Narcissistic literary or musical giants are insufferably vain. Richard Wagner, the nineteenth-century composer, wrote, "The world ought to give me what I need. Is it an unheard of demand if I hold that the little luxury I like is my due? I who am procuring enjoyment to the world and to thousands."[1]

Here are key ingredients for what makes big shots tick:

1. They like to make powerful first impressions.

2. They give constant attention to how they look, what they wear, and what they say.

3. Their time is valuable. Others should give them the right of way in traffic, allow them to cut in lines, and serve them immediately in restaurants. They are VIPs.

4. At work they should be exempted from difficult or dull tasks. They need special assignments that lead to recognition.

5. Their inalienable rights are greater than those of others. People should be happy to wait on them, follow their lead, and take their advice.

6. No one has a right to criticize them. It is understandable if they react with anger at such insolence.

7. Others should be glad to give to them without expecting anything in return.

8. They are so unique that others should help them financially without expecting to be paid back.

9. They enjoy daydreams and fantasies of success, glory, wealth, and love.

One narcissistic physician bragged about how he was going to start a chain of fifteen hundred clinics around the country. He said he would become a legend in medical history. As it turned out, he eventually had his medical license revoked for overmedicating patients.

BETWEEN MAN AND WOMAN

I spoke to a women's group on personality patterns of men. After the seminar, Jennifer asked me about her boyfriend's behavior.

"He picks all the places we go," she said. "He picks me up late without apologizing, and he ignores me when he talks to other people. He talks about himself all the time and never asks about me. He even announced that we were going to be engaged without asking me!"

I couldn't help smiling. "Your boyfriend is a dyed-in-the-wool narcissist," I said. "If he's unwilling to change, you're seeing the bottom line of the relationship right now. There'll always be just two people in the relationship—him and him."

She looked disappointed. "But he's so cute!" she said.

"Jennifer," I said, "that's his hook. He relies on his good looks because he believes that he is God's gift to women. He feels entitled to special treatment forever. He's the flame and you're the moth, and that's that!"

Personality wholeness enables us to be our own best selves. People who honor God's psychology find freedom and spontaneity, just as Jesus had in His earthly life.

"It seems cruel to judge him," she said.

"I'm not judging him," I replied. "I'm describing his real behavior, according to what you've told me. There are many hidden payoffs for being a narcissist, and one of them is having an attractive woman like you dangling on his arm. He gives you a little attention, and your role is to show gratitude that he gives you the time of day."

Jennifer said, "That's exactly what he does!"

I gave Jennifer an impromptu homework assignment. "The next time you walk through a mall together, notice what happens if you stand in front of a mirror. Narcissistic big shots will see only themselves. Even if you have your hair done, your makeup perfect, and a stunning new dress, you will be invisible to him. He'll comb his hair or straighten his shirt. He won't notice you."

She gasped. "Dr. Montgomery, that happened this afternoon! We were standing in front of a mirror together. I was thinking how nice we looked as a couple. He ran a comb through his hair and said, 'Awesome.' He didn't even see me!"

The Little King

Spouses often describe living with big shots as a love-hate relationship. They feel taken in by the airs of self-importance, yet put down by the selfishness of the big shot. Narcissistic big shots have no interest in the desires of their spouses.

A young wife named Sally said of her husband, "Our home is centered on his comforts and desires. He plays the stereo as loud as he wants and chooses the selections without ever asking me. We watch his shows on television and go to his favorite movies. I cook what he wants to eat, no matter what I'm in the mood for. He's the little king, and I'm his live-in maid!"

Sally was accurately describing the big shot pattern—they literally live at the center of the universe as they know it. They flout the rules of shared living, thinking only about what they want.

Big shots constantly compete with their spouses. Whether they play tennis, golf, or bridge, they must win. If spouses receive an award or an honor, they feel jealous. If her husband makes a point in a group conversation, the narcissistic wife will feel compelled to one-up him. As one narcissistic wife told me, "I'm the spotlight. He's the footlight."

Multiple divorces or sudden breakups are common among big shots, especially if both partners play the narcissistic role. That is the fate of so many Hollywood marriages because neither person can stand being in the background.

SEX IN MARRIAGE

Since big shots thrive on self-importance and self-indulgence, they use sex as a way to show how well they can perform. They'll wonder how many orgasms they can have and how else the partner can please them.

The spouse of a big shot may complain that she feels that her partner is masturbating, using her body. A pastor's wife said to me, "My husband's been having sex with me for twenty years. He says that he's highly skilled at lovemaking. But love has nothing to do with it. He just uses me, rolls over, and goes to sleep!"

THOUGHT PATTERNS

Big shots have such an inflated view of themselves that everyone else is inferior. Here's what their automatic self-talk sounds like:

- I'm superior to others, and they should acknowledge this fact.

- I must do whatever I can to reinforce my superior status and to expand my personal domain.

> *A single word that captures narcissistic thinking is entitled.*

- People should realize that I deserve special treatment.
- I'm entitled to admiration with no extra effort on my part.
- If you love me, you'll do whatever I want.
- I have no use for people who don't hold me in the highest esteem.
- All that matters is what I want or what I think.

Big shots tend to exaggerate their abilities and inflate their self-image in the eyes of others. A single word that captures narcissistic thinking is *entitled*.

EMOTIONAL LIFE

Big shots are emotionally cool, calm, and collected. They want to appear unshakable, as captains of destiny and queens of poise.

> *Big shots want to appear unshakable, as captains of destiny and queens of poise.*

Actually, they are cool because they're impervious to the needs of others.

When others aren't spellbound by their presence, big shots can pull back into icy silence or give the cold shoulder. This is a manipulative ploy, for they are really saying, "If you don't worship my presence, I'll withdraw my glory and punish you with my absence."

Self-indulgence can lead to reliance on alcohol or drugs to enhance feelings of grandiosity. Some big shots have reported to me that they like to get high alone so that they are not bothered by lesser mortals. Under the influence, they feel transfigured with fantasies of personal glory. Also, negative experiences or emotions can be smoothed over with a few drinks. Big shots believe that they're too smart to become chemically addicted, which sets them up for addiction. The warm glow of a chemical high can become a permanent substitute for relating to others with real feelings.

Though presenting an unflappable exterior, big shots are often troubled by depression and an inner sense of barrenness. They become restless if they fail or if the real world doesn't give them what they believe they deserve. Rather than facing weak feelings and confiding in others, they tend to lie about shortcomings to bolster the illusion of perpetual success.

PERCEPTION OF GOD

Big shots believe that they are God's gift to the world: "God thinks that I'm the greatest person He ever created. He is impressed by my talents and recognizes my outstanding attributes. He has endowed me considerably beyond ordinary people."

Big shots usually have an exceptionally shallow prayer life. They pray mainly for success, fame, and wealth. If you approach them with a need, they feel put upon, wondering why you can't handle it yourself. The big shot's perception of God is contaminated by his or her need to play God Junior. Big shots thrive on self-glorification while pretending to give the glory to God.

Narcissistic ministers buy expensive cars and showy clothes, and they take first-class vacations with money from their flocks. They brag about their prosperity as a sign of how highly God regards them. They promise to make you rich, too, if only you'll pledge them your money as proof of your faith in God.

Narcissists in general see themselves as entitled to God's special favor. They automatically presume that their goals and needs are synonymous with God's will.

GROWTH AND CHANGE

For big shots, growth in God's psychology begins by stepping down off the pedestal. As Jesus frees them from their needs for one-upmanship, they can build friendships based on mutuality.

Big shots need skills of active listening and a new sensitivity in place of preoccupation with themselves—this is the love compass point. They need to admit their weakness and make amends when they've been too self-serving—this is the weakness compass point. Activating the assertion compass point, they develop discipline and perseverance, working for competence instead of resting on supposed laurels.

With the help of her colleagues and daily prayer, Kathy learned to be a team player. She grew to enjoy working with Emily and Peggy instead of competing with them. She accepted critical feedback instead of seeing herself as being above criticism. She discovered the inner satisfaction of sharing accomplishments with others. Kathy began giving compliments to others. She could acknowledge their greater wisdom in certain areas. At last she felt the comfort of a warm companionship with fellow human beings.

PRACTICAL GROWTH STEPS

1. Become willing to face that underneath your cool facade, you experience anxiety around others as soon as the spotlight is taken off you. Notice when you become instantly bored because you're not receiving admiration. Accept that in spite of your inflated image of yourself, many people sense how empty you are inside and how you think of no one but yourself.

2. This month practice deliberately moving the spotlight of attention and conversation from yourself to others. Handle the temporary insecurity you feel by telling yourself that other people are just as interesting as you are, and it's time to find out about them.

Use your charisma to show genuine interest in what they're saying and what they're feeling. Resist the temptation to take back the limelight. Really listen to them instead of thinking about what you want to say next to impress them. Give up your need to impress others.

Relax. If you are really interested in others, they will feel it and reciprocate. But if you come barreling through with more narcissistic statements, they will unconsciously turn a deaf ear.

3. Talk over with some friends how they really perceive you. Be ready to accept what they say instead of denying it. Then tell them that you are tired of being conceited and arrogant.

Ask them to help you change by showing you how to talk about deeper feelings. Share your anxieties and bouts of depression, and laugh at yourself when you get on your high horse. There is nothing quite so healing as healthy humor—calling yourself on your pretenses—and nothing quite so endearing as revealing your shortcomings.

4. Take these Scriptures to heart and pray for sustained guidance in your personality transformation from a self-centered person to a caring human being.

> For people will be lovers of themselves, lovers of money, boasters, arrogant (2 Tim. 3:2 NRSV).

> Woe to those who are wise in their own eyes,
> And prudent in their own sight! (Isa. 5:21).

> And I will say to my soul, "Soul, you have many goods laid up for many years; take your ease; eat, drink, and be merry." But God said to him, "Fool! This night your soul will be required of you; then whose will those things be which you have provided?" (Luke 12:19–20).

> He is proud, knowing nothing, but is obsessed with disputes and arguments over words, from which come envy, strife, reviling, evil suspicions, useless wranglings of men of corrupt minds and destitute of the truth, who suppose that godliness is a means of gain. From such withdraw yourself (1 Tim. 6:4–5).

> Let nothing be done through selfish ambition or conceit, but in lowliness of mind let each esteem others better than himself (Phil. 2:3).

Let this mind be in you which was also in Christ Jesus, who, being in the form of God, did not consider it robbery to be equal with God, but made Himself of no reputation, taking the form of a bondservant, and coming in the likeness of men. And being found in appearance as a man, He humbled Himself and became obedient to the point of death, even the death of the cross (Phil. 2:5–8).

If we are living now by the Holy Spirit's power, let us follow the Holy Spirit's leading in every part of our lives. Then we won't need to look for honors and popularity, which lead to jealousy and hard feelings (Gal. 5:25 TLB).

Therefore humble yourselves under the mighty hand of God, that He may exalt you in due time (1 Peter 5:6).

5. Give up your need for privileged treatment. Ask God to help you cultivate a spirit of outgoing love, a spontaneous altruism that is real. Put new emphasis on supporting, helping, and assisting others.

Help a person who is having car trouble, take a gift to a neighbor who has just moved in, welcome newcomers at your church or social club, graciously yield in traffic situations, or help a college student pay tuition. Their appreciation will come back to you in terms of genuine affection and admiration.

CHAPTER 10

Perfectionists

"Not by might nor by power, but by My Spirit,"
Says the Lord *of hosts.*

—Zechariah 4:6

I received my Ph.D. in my late twenties, the youngest in the graduating class. I'd read nearly a thousand books and felt proud of my accomplishments. Within the next few years, I published my first two books. While I was wise in my own eyes, in truth, I was a pain to be around.

I was hired as the director of group therapy in a psychiatric ward. I planned to fix everyone—and quickly. I gave lectures to the group to show them how much I knew. I offered advice to show how clever I was. I was the man to save the world.

I'd been there about two months when an older man named Bill said, "Dr. Montgomery, you've got a big ego. It really gets in your way."

I was stunned. How dare he analyze me!

A female member of the group asked if they could talk about me for a change.

I was miffed, but I decided to help them out by listening. That day the group came alive for the first time. They exposed in a flash my idealized image of a know-it-all with a Messiah complex.

"You haven't ever shown empathy for my pain," Sally said. "You're so obsessed with trying to control us that you're not a real person."

"You need to fix everybody to show us how great you are!" said Bill.

"Doctor, you need some humility," seconded Sam.

On and on they talked, agreeing with each other's comments and adding to them. I was sweating and blushing, sometimes trying to defend myself and sometimes listening with disbelief. Finally, I looked at the clock with relief. "It's time to wind up," I said, hoping to shut them up and leave with a shred of dignity.

"Dr. Montgomery," said Sam, "I want to say one last thing."

"Okay, Sam, go ahead," I said.

"For these past two months you've been a jerk."

I left the group feeling shattered. I had entered the room the wise doctor, sent by God to save these people. Now I didn't know who I was. Worse yet, I recognized some truth in what they said. That night I wanted to resign from the hospital and leave the planet. But I decided to pray instead. I poured out my hurt and anger to the Lord. After I'd finishing venting, a still, small voice spoke inside me: *Keep going back, Dan. You'll learn a lot.*

Reluctantly, I went back to the next group session. I told the people I'd been shaken by what they'd shared. I could hear the pain in my voice. "I'm tired of defending myself," I said. "And I'm tired of being a know-it-all. I'm going to let more of my real self out in this group. I want to learn something, too."

"Thank God!" cried one woman. Then she quit focusing on me and started sharing her pain. I felt empathy toward her for the first time.

What astonished me was that in the weeks to come, we became colearners in the art of living. My professional input was more tempered with self-disclosures about my flaws and foibles. After several months, Bill told me that sharing my weaknesses more openly had become my greatest strength.

I've never forgotten the growth process modeled in that group—love and assertion, weakness and strength. They helped me to take growth stretches I never dreamed possible instead of remaining a stodgy and wooden perfectionist.

WHAT MAKES PERFECTIONISTS TICK?

Do you know any dictatorial business executives who demand a perfectly efficient organization, even though it mangles the people who work there? Do you work in a place where there is an obsession with production, but people's feelings are ignored? A waitress told me the other day that managers were always making rigid rules without ever consulting the ones who knew the customers best—the waiters and waitresses.

What about compulsive types in churches? They are know-it-alls who constantly judge other people. Psychologist Adrian van Kaam writes, "I continually drive myself to increasing religious perfection and regularity, to more and more magnificent manifestations of apostolic fervor, in order to display my superiority in saintliness. . . . I may believe that my remarkable regularity is the fruit of holiness."[1]

Do you remember that controlling teacher who forced you to memorize tons of trivia and regurgitate it on rigorous objective tests? One who gave too much homework, was too long-winded, and stifled your creativity and imagination?

How about a compulsive parent who turns a home into a museum showcase? Everything must stay perfectly in place. Everyone must play a prescribed role. Family members are constantly chided for being messy, being late, or adopting nonconventional values.

> *Perfectionists live under the curse of perfectionism and are driven by the tyranny of the shoulds.*

Compulsive perfectionists use willpower and discipline to achieve goals, but they are out of touch with their emotions and bodies. Key words for compulsive perfectionists are *control* and *should*. To them, orderliness is godliness. They live under the curse of perfectionism and are driven by the tyranny of the shoulds.

Here is what makes perfectionists tick:

1. They believe that work, duty, and moral perfection are the most important things in life. They emphasize self-discipline, emotional restraint, and the letter of the law.

2. They are preoccupied with how life should be. They're uncomfortable with how life really is.

3. They are reluctant to admit mistakes, say when they don't know something, ask for help, or say they're sorry.

4. They insist that subordinates—who may include spouses, children, and employees—adhere to established rules and methods.

5. They view the world in terms of rules, time schedules, and social convention. They resist novel ideas or anything unfamiliar.

6. They are so nitpicky about procedures that they often miss the bigger picture.

7. They are so focused on what seems right to them that they are oblivious to others' needs and feelings.

8. They are workaholics, because they have difficulty taking vacations or having fun.

9. They are close-minded, yet remain convinced they know everything.

BETWEEN MAN AND WOMAN

The perfectionistic spouse turns a marriage into more of a parent-to-child than an adult-to-adult relationship. The compulsive partner constantly seeks to reform the mate by disapproving, scolding, and "shoulding."

An interest in thoroughness, details, and practical procedures leads perfectionists to lecture spouses:

- "Don't you know that those colors you're wearing don't match?"
- "Can't you put anything back after you've used it?"
- "How many times do I have to tell you . . ."
- "You should know better than that!"
- "Your shoes are out of order in the closet again!"

Perfectionists view marriage as a contract to which they have honorably given their word. Duty is a concept they understand, but having fun is not. As soon as they say, "I do," perfectionists take over with their demands and expectations. They are resistant to a partner's input unless it conforms to their conventional understanding of husband and wife roles.

Perfectionists live in the mind and tune out the heart and body. They want to control the marriage, not experience its romance and adventure. But this cerebral approach can be deadly to a marriage because joy and pleasure are systematically squeezed out.

SEX IN MARRIAGE

The perfectionist's approach to sex lacks spontaneity, warmth, and playfulness. The couple's sex life can become overly regimented.

Compulsive perfectionists seek a predictable routine for sexual intercourse. There is little interest in pleasuring the spouse or experimenting with sexual positions. As one woman said, "The missionary position on Tuesday and Thursday nights under the covers with the bedroom lights out is his favorite."

Perfectionists are usually uncomfortable with their bodies and with nudity. "It seems improper for my husband to see me naked," said a woman. "Sex is for procreation, not for personal entertainment."

Another aspect of compulsive control is having criteria that the partner must meet before sex can happen. If the partner misses one step, he rolls over and says, "Sorry, not tonight." A woman said, "First, I have to say and do everything right for the whole day before the night that I want sex. Next, I have to give him a massage for about thirty minutes. Then, I have to say the right words about what a good and successful husband he is. If I do everything right, which is about one time out of five, we'll have one brief moment of pleasure."

THOUGHT PATTERN

These automatic thoughts characterize the perfectionist personality pattern:

- Be a pillar of strength and strive at all times to demonstrate that you are in control.
- An orderly home and work environment are musts.
- Be decisive in practical affairs.
- Never shrink from your duty.
- Push yourself and others toward excellence and perfection.
- Criticize others to help them avoid future mistakes.
- Follow the rule book.

Perfectionists perceive other people as too casual, irresponsible, self-indulgent, or incompetent.

EMOTIONAL LIFE

Underneath the strong facade, perfectionists are indecisive. They have deep anxieties about being found wanting. These feelings can originate in a home where criticism and anger are camouflaged behind a pretense of love and propriety. The parents turn every experience into a lesson to be learned or a moral to be taught. The child becomes conditioned to black-and-white responses of right and wrong, and judges emotions rather than experiences them.

> *Underneath the strong facade, perfectionists are indecisive.*

Mark told me how he loved baseball as a young child until his father got involved. His dad bought an expensive bat and glove and made the boy practice with him for three hours every evening all summer. On Saturdays, they'd play up to eight hours. "If you're going to play baseball, son," his dad always said, "you're going to do it right and be the best!"

Clay became a heavyweight boxing champion of the Marine Corps. Yet he suffered from great anxiety underneath his confidence. He told me that the only time he was knocked out was the night that his father came to a fight. The dad sat in a ringside seat and kept yelling orders to his son. "Keep your left up, son. Watch out for his uppercut. Quit shuffling your feet." Clay was knocked out in the first round because his dad's "shoulds" broke his natural rhythm.

A fifty-year-old woman named Helen paid her mother's airplane fare from another state to see Helen give the commencement address at her Ph.D. graduation from Harvard. Faculty members came up afterward to praise Helen's speech. When her mother came forward, Helen's heart beat fast in anticipation. Her mother exclaimed, "I felt so ashamed of your weight that I didn't hear anything you said. And that dress is awful!"

It's no wonder that the emotional life of perfectionists has dried up long ago.

From Anxiety to Judgment

Compulsive perfectionists counter their deep-seated anxiety by becoming judgmental. They don't know how to hang loose or have a good belly laugh. Instead, they're tense and self-righteous.

Perfectionists pooh-pooh the value of feelings. But the truth is that they are so emotionally underdeveloped, they don't know how feelings work. Devoid of emotional intuition, they're in the dark when it comes to other people's feelings. So they analyze and judge instead. Unknowingly, they blank out the feelings that enhance and endear relationships.

Their secret anxiety is reflected in a chronic fear that "if I don't have everything under control, life will fall apart." They come across emotionally as more negative than positive because they're always looking for things to go wrong. When life is less than perfect, they conclude that things are out of control. Since life can never be perfect, they're always on edge.

Perfectionists display awkward contradictions. They tend to be standoffish, even though they want to be admired. They are stingy, even though they see themselves as generous. They have trouble giving compliments because they feel in secret competition with others.

PERCEPTION OF GOD

Perfectionists believe that God is perfect, and that He demands conformity and punishes anything less than perfection. Self-control is the paramount issue in religious life. The Bible or the church must be followed to the letter. Achieving moral perfection and correcting those who err are ways to serve God.

Having lost sensitivity to the gentle prompting of the Holy Spirit, they may seek to accomplish worthy goals, yet inflict pain on others while doing so. Their obsession with detail prevents them from grasping God's bigger picture, and they miss out on love, play, and humor.

It may take the threat of divorce, a near fatal car accident, a child gone astray, or a heart attack to jar compulsive perfectionists into the awareness that they are mere mortals. This awakening can be a blessing used by God to slow them down and teach them to lean on Jesus.

GROWTH AND CHANGE

Larry was a bright boy who grew up in an affluent home. His father, a prominent surgeon, provided his family with a beautiful home, expensive cars, and designer clothes. Larry's father was a respected man in his church and community, and Larry idolized him. Larry determined to be at the head of his class, just like his father—always in control, just like his father.

But Larry seldom saw his father, who would leave for hospital rounds before his family got up and seldom returned before Larry's bedtime. Larry knew his father best from the achievement awards on his father's den wall. His mother slept in most mornings, often complaining about not feeling well.

When Larry was ten, he heard his parents arguing, something they seldom did. His father angrily complained that the house was a complete mess with dishes piled in the sink most of the time. Larry heard his mother defend herself: "I need more help. It's hard raising Larry all by myself. You're never home to see what it's like!" A housekeeper arrived the next day. But Larry's mother remained much the same.

One day Larry overheard the housekeeper gossiping on the phone: "This woman's a real lush, I tell you. Larry survived on his own peanut butter and jelly sandwiches for years. I'm surprised he didn't starve before I came." As he listened, hot humiliation spread through Larry's body and his mind raced. *My mother is a drunk!* he thought. *Who else knows? Does Dad know?*

Larry knew what he had to do. He had to get the housekeeper fired. He had to protect the family's reputation. He had to take charge.

By the time Larry was twelve, he had become adept at taking care of the house. He waited on his mother when she didn't feel well. He made excuses for her behavior when friends came over.

To outsiders, he thought, everything looked normal. Larry became a strong child who kept the family together.

Larry completed high school and college with top grades, allowing him to follow in his father's footsteps by graduating from medical school. He was anxious to move ahead rapidly. But the work in his residency was demanding. He had to give up much of his self-appointed supervision of his mother. Months went by without contact from his father.

He volunteered for extra hours beyond the impossibly long shifts of his regular assignments. Larry didn't want to miss anything that might keep him ahead of the pack. He considered himself far superior to his fellows.

Larry was lucky. When his overconfidence and exhaustion caused him to miscalculate a dosage on a patient's prescription, a young nurse named Jennie caught his error in time. But he responded with anger—anger at himself for his mistake, and resentment toward her for pointing it out.

Jennie was impressed by his dedication. At the same time she was sure that another disaster was waiting to happen. In helping him, she felt a bond between them grow.

She knew he'd been watching her, too. But his watching had taken on a new character. He was surly and demanding, looking for mistakes he seemed sure she was making.

She finally confronted him with her frustration: "You've been on my back for weeks now, and I know I don't deserve it."

Larry relented after more arguing, and he apologized to her, explaining how important his medical career was to him.

Jennie told him that she admired his expertise and commitment.

Larry needed to hear that from her. He told her all his dreams and plans. She seemed as interested in them as he was.

They saw each other regularly. Within a few months, he asked her to marry him. Then their conflicts began again. She wanted to continue her career so they could work together. He wanted her to quit even before they were married.

"It costs money to start a medical practice. We need my income," Jennie argued.

"Your income is nothing," Larry shouted. "I don't need your income. Besides, wives of professional men don't work. It's demeaning."

"I'm a professional, too," Jennie responded with hurt in her voice.

"I can take care of my career and our finances too. I want my wife to take care of herself."

Larry really wanted Jennie as his wife, but she kept resisting his carefully laid plans for their life. The harder he tried to make her understand, the more stubborn she became. He was having problems with his career, too, but he couldn't share them with her. He was sure he would lose her if he shared with her his problems in getting a large enough loan to start his practice.

Larry visited his mother one afternoon, and he confessed all his problems to her. It was quite a role reversal. He had spent years protecting her, and he was parading all his fears in front of her.

"Larry, I've been thinking about how much responsibility you've had to carry all alone since you were a young child. I feel sorry about it. I want you to know how much I care for you and appreciate your strength. I want to do something for you now, but I have to have your promise that you'll accept it before I tell you what it is."

With much puzzlement and some protest, Larry finally promised. To his extreme surprise, she said, "I want you to join a therapy group. I'll pay. I think it's time you found out that others have something to offer."

GROWTH THROUGH WEAKNESS

Larry was willing to talk in the group I was leading. He explained that he was there to please his mother. He dazzled the group with stories about medicine, with himself in the starring role.

One of the group members asked, "Do bad things ever happen, even when you're strong?"

Thoughts of Jennie came rushing into Larry's head. He shifted in his chair, looking down at the carpet. "When you're strong, you can control things, have them your way," Larry responded.

"What about people? Can you always control people?" I asked.

"If you're strong enough, I suppose you can," he mumbled.

I had an idea. "Larry, would you be willing to try an experiment with the group? It has to do with strength and weakness."

"That depends," he said hesitantly.

"It's really simple," I said. "You're a strong man physically. All you have to do is lie on the floor. Four of us will position ourselves by your arms and legs to try and hold you down. You try to get up. I want you to find out if strength can always control things and, if it can't, what it feels like to really be helpless."

Larry smiled broadly. "Oh, is that all? I'm pretty strong physically. I don't think just four of you can hold me down."

"That's fine," I said. "I want you to know that this is just an exercise, though. If you want to stop, let us know and we will."

"Got it," Larry said with the same smile.

After Larry lay on the carpet, a volunteer got in position at each arm and leg. "All right, Larry, get up," I said.

Larry strained with all his might, turning red in the face. But the group members exerted equal pressure downward and held him firm. After a minute or so, he relaxed to catch his breath. Then he squirmed and twisted with full strength to raise himself up again, but he was unable to budge. This pattern was repeated several more times.

Larry wasn't laughing. He tried to buck them off with a surge of desperation. His arms and legs trembled; his breathing was labored. He had overestimated his strength. He looked scared and ashamed. Suddenly, he began to cry, quietly at first, then in huge, deep sobs that seemed to come from way down inside him. I told the group to let him up, and they helped him to his feet.

Larry sat down and began to talk about what he had just learned.

"I was thinking of my fiancée," he said. "I think she's been trying to tell me for a long time that I need to back off and quit trying so hard. I've been trying to control her and to be strong for her. It almost broke us up. I've been hitting a lot of brick walls lately." He teared up again, this time with a relaxed smile. "I think I got the message. I have a peaceful feeling inside. I can't wait to see Jennie!"

Weakness and vulnerability are occasions to draw near to God for comfort and encouragement. God is far more accepting of real weaknesses than compulsive perfectionists realize. The God of the Bible is not a compulsive perfectionist, a workaholic, a harsh taskmaster, or a "shoulding" tyrant. God appreciates the uniqueness of persons. If you trust God's psychology, He'll bring out your inner beauty.

> *God is far more accepting of real weaknesses than perfectionists realize.*

PRACTICAL GROWTH STRETCHES

1. Accept at the outset that you have little experiential knowledge of love and grace. As a result, you have reached the erroneous conclusion that achievement, perfection, and control are the

goals of life. Wrong. Love and grace are the ways to inner and outer fulfillment of the will of God.

The first growth stretch is to honestly confess to Jesus that you desire a deeper, transforming experience of His love and grace. Ask the Holy Spirit to help you fall in love with Jesus. Then make a commitment to open more of your real feelings in a prayerful dialogue with God. You do not need to do more for the kingdom of God. You need to do less and enjoy it more.

Practice laughing at your mistakes this week, letting your schedule slide if it means helping someone else, and talking more openly about your old needs for perfection and how they never allow you to be joyous or free.

2. Challenge your attitudes of superiority when they manifest themselves. You must face your hidden competitiveness, jealousy, and envy of other people's achievements or good fortune.

Practice spreading compliments, praise, and joy about others' accomplishments this week. Learn to genuinely build people up. Realize that you are in no way diminished when someone else succeeds. Offer support, encouragement, and kind words, and quit being so self-centered.

3. When someone criticizes you or tries to give you feedback, don't automatically justify yourself and get huffy. Give up your defense mechanism of denial by humbly agreeing with your needs for growth.

Honestly integrate people's constructive input. Ask for more perceptual feedback from friends and loved ones this week: "How do you really see me? Am I compulsive to a fault? Is it true that I'm tense, grim, and nitpicky?" When they give you an honest answer, don't argue.

Thank them for their candor, and tell them of your aims to develop wholeness. Let them know that you wish to become more playful and loving.

4. Type or write out these Scriptures and put copies on your bathroom mirror, on your desktop, and by your bed. Ask God to help you lighten up and find your way to health and happiness.

Humble yourselves under the mighty hand of God, that He may exalt you in due time, casting all your care upon Him, for He cares for you (1 Peter 5:6–7).

Be of the same mind toward one another. Do not set your mind on high things, but associate with the humble. Do not be wise in your own opinion (Rom. 12:16).

For all these worldly things, these evil desires—. . . the pride that comes from wealth and importance—these are not from God (1 John 2:16 TLB).

Why do you judge your brother? Or why do you show contempt for your brother? For we shall all stand before the judgment seat of Christ (Rom. 14:10).

And why quibble about the speck in someone else's eye—his little fault—when a board is in your own? . . . Hypocrite! First get rid of the board, and then perhaps you can see well enough to deal with his speck! (Luke 6:41–42 TLB).

Therefore most gladly I will rather boast in my infirmities, that the power of Christ may rest upon me. . . . For *when I am weak, then I am strong* (2 Cor. 12:9–10, italics mine).

The sacrifices of God are a broken spirit,
A broken and a contrite heart—
These, O God, You will not despise (Ps. 51:17).

5. Do three things that are frivolous, silly, and spontaneous this week. Swing on a park swing; give someone an African violet; give your spouse a massage; buy a family game and make some popcorn; buy a nontraditional outfit; go to lunch with the gang; take a day off and snooze or watch videos.

Realize that the best contributions you can make have to do with being warm, spontaneous, and accepting of people's differences.

PART 3

Virtues of God's Psychology

I am the vine, you are the branches. He who abides in Me, and I in him, bears much fruit; for without Me you can do nothing.

—Jesus
John 15:5

CHAPTER 11

Purifying Your Personality

[I] will refine them as silver is refined,
And test them as gold is tested.
They will call on My name,
And I will answer them.
I will say, "This is My people";
And each one will say, "The LORD is my God."

—Zechariah 13:9

Fran was the head of a department whose company had hired me to do a series of team-building consultations. A tall woman with thick-rimmed glasses, Fran impressed me with her serious demeanor and intelligence. We set up a series of training sessions to help people work more harmoniously with each other.

Minutes before the first session, Fran called me into her office. "Dr. Montgomery," she said crisply, "I'd like you to change people's attitudes so that they're more obedient to authority. I want them to do what I say so we can get along better."

During the first morning, I presented the principles of God's psychology as they apply to team building in a corporate setting. I mentioned that healthy interpersonal relationships require openness, trust, and acceptance of people's strengths and weaknesses. I went over the eight partial patterns of personality, sharing some of my shortcomings, and I showed how each pattern sabotages an effective team environment. That afternoon I asked volunteers to disclose what they'd learned about themselves. To my surprise, Fran's hand went up first.

"I feel embarrassed saying this, but I expected Dr. Montgomery to tell us how to better follow rules and regulations. Instead, he talked about our personalities. I've discovered some real problems with mine. I think I'm a weird combination of a compulsive perfectionist and an avoidant wallflower."

Fran shifted in her seat and took a deep breath. "I've got so much anxiety about being perfect that I end up judging all of you. But I'm also avoidant because I always feel strained and self-conscious around people. I'm so afraid of being judged less than perfect that I don't let anybody get to know me," said Fran, tears forming in her eyes.

The group gave Fran a round of applause for the courage she'd shown. I felt encouraged because when leaders begin to change, organizations are freed for growth.

Fran made an appointment for individual counseling. At the first session, she had just returned from a family trip to Disney World. Her ten-year-old son David had created a major scene. Toward the end of the day, David had wrapped his arms around a lamppost, kicking and screaming at anyone who tried to budge him. He threw an hour-long temper tantrum. Fran pleaded and threatened to no avail.

"How can I control David in a situation like that?" she asked.

"I think the problem is that you're trying to control him too much already. I wonder if you listen to his wants and needs. Did you ask him what he'd like to do at Disney World?" I asked.

Her face went blank and she bit her lower lip. "No, it never occurred to me. I organized the whole day and kept the family on schedule."

Fran prided herself on her conscientious approach to work and family life. But she admitted not knowing the first thing about how she or anyone else really felt. Her rigid pattern of following rules and regulations broke down whenever a situation called for intuition or emotional sensitivity.

During our next session, Fran spoke of a repeating dream she'd had for the past few months. "In the dream, I'm a little girl who lives in a town of the Old West where the sheriff and judge are the same man. He's a hanging judge who has so many rules that nobody can keep them all. Every weekend he finds someone guilty of breaking a rule and hangs the person in the town plaza. In the dream I'm scared to death he's going to hang me." Her face paled as she spoke, her hands trembling slightly.

"Fran, can you see that the hanging judge personifies your perfectionism?" I asked. "Inside your personality there's no room for weakness or failure. Only harsh judgments that leave you in constant fear. You can't relax and just be human. You're afraid the hanging judge will get you."

Her eyes widened. "My gosh! You mean part of me is the hanging judge and the other part is the scared little girl?"

"Exactly. Your strength and weakness compass points are at war with each other, and neither one can win. I call this the self-torture game. Your perfectionist side says, 'You've got to shape up or ship out,' and your wallflower side feels shamed and rejected."

"How on earth can I get over this?" she asked. "I've been like this since childhood."

"You need to accept yourself as an imperfect human being with fears and failings. It's normal to feel helpless now and then without making a big deal about it. Why don't we pray for God to help you get rid of the hanging judge and accept your whole self, strengths and weaknesses together?"

"Let's do," she said as she nodded.

When we had finished praying, I suggested a homework assignment.

"Picture a scale from one to ten," I said. "Ten stands for perfection and one stands for failure. How do you judge most people?"

She smiled and shook her head. "I want them all to be tens, but since nobody makes it, I judge them as ones."

"That's what I thought," I said. "That's how your hanging judge controls your relationships. So here's the growth stretch. This week tell yourself that if people make an average score of five, you'll accept them. And if the hanging judge makes a fuss, tell him he's fired."

A week later Fran came to our session with a notepad. She had kept tabs on the homework assignment. She said, "I listened to my inner voices all week. My hanging judge wanted to judge people for being less than perfect a total of thirty-seven times. But I kept telling that voice in my head he was fired. I practiced lowering my standard for acceptance to a five and every single person passed. I feel relieved. People seem friendlier, too."

After a couple of months, Fran was using her self compass in a more successful way. She could cheer people up, forgive more easily, and feel caring for those around her (love). When she needed to assert herself, she did so with greater diplomacy, listening to other people's feelings and respecting their points of view (assertion). She could admit a shortcoming, make an apology, and experience humility without feeling humiliated (weakness). Her strength shifted from an obsession with dictatorial control to more cooperation and respect for individual differences (strength). The LAWS of God's psychology were working.

In our last session, Fran's body had relaxed considerably. "I realize I'm never going to be perfect, but now I have a better goal," she said. "With God's help, I want to enjoy life and people, not stand around and judge."

My consultation with Fran's department continued for six months. As Fran developed her whole self, the group developed transparency, caring, and esprit de corps. At the end of the six months, the hanging judge was removed from Fran's personality, and the rope around the department's neck disappeared. God's psychology was helping them find their way to health and happiness.

GOD WORKS WITHIN OUR PERSONALITIES

God works through our free choices to transform our personalities. No matter how we are blocked, God's psychology helps us make progress toward psychological and spiritual wholeness.

> *God works through our free choices to transform our personalities.*

Personality wholeness enables us to be our own best selves—with more excitement and less misery than one-sidedness can ever bring. People who honor God's psychology find freedom and spontaneity, just as Jesus had in His earthly life.

We need a combination of faith and action for carrying out the process of personality transformation. Faith orients us with positive expectations about how God and caring others can help us make gradual progress toward wholeness. Action means

- taking responsibility.
- facing our deepest fears.
- praying for help when we need it.
- reaching out to help others.

> *We need a combination of faith and action for carrying out the process of personality transformation.*

- following our inner truth in Christ.
- making decisions and taking stands.
- making amends when we've overstepped our bounds.

We need God because we need an intelligence greater than our own to show us the way through life, a love greater than our own to combat our fears, and a personality more whole than our own to heal and comfort us. His ways are higher than our ways.

VIRTUES OF GOD'S PSYCHOLOGY

As soon as we use the self compass, former negative patterns are redeemed for virtue. We humbly admit our need for personal growth. We apply the principles of God's psychology. Our shortcomings are gradually transformed into these positive virtues:

- Clinging Vine—*virtue of charity.* Sensitive and sympathetic. Doesn't need the limelight. A good listener and follower. Tender and talented in care for children. Quick to forgive. Compromises easily. Is kind and helpful.

- Prima Donna—*virtue of good cheer.* Makes life exciting, colorful, and humorous. Loves to laugh and play. Gregarious. Doesn't take the world too seriously. Feels buoyant and lighthearted most of the time. Always ready for an adventure or surprise.

- Bully—*virtue of courage.* A master of debate and rhetoric. Not intimidated by anyone. Able to hold up under stress. Good at confrontation and challenging unfairness. A fearless negotiator.

- Con Artist—*virtue of creativity*. Risk taking. Inventive and imaginative. Nonconforming. Knows how to cut through red tape. Gives novel responses to new or difficult situations. Is not intimidated by threats or punishment, which only makes for more resourcefulness.

- Wallflower—*virtue of empathy*. Isn't demanding or competitive. Sensitive rapport with others. Peacemaking. Has a high frustration tolerance. Not motivated by status or material gain. Is especially tender toward children, animals, and those who suffer.

- Hermit—*virtue of objectivity*. Lives and lets live. Can be fair-minded and impartial. Separates facts from feelings. Responds to emergencies with calm detachment. Not burdened by other people's expectations. Doesn't need to impress anyone. Inner directed.

- Perfectionist—*virtue of discipline*. Conscientious, industrious, and reliable. Values self-discipline and stick-to-itiveness. Endorses social conventions and proprieties. Pillar of the community. Emphasizes rationality and logic. Champion of morality. Carrier of tradition.

- Big Shot—*virtue of autonomy*. Self-governing and self-confident. Optimistic. Marches to own tune and not the drumbeat of others. Easily assumes leadership. Takes pride in achievements and personal poise.

These positive virtues can surface only when we choose to live by the principles of God's psychology rather than merely exist through our partial patterns. The rhythmic and self-correcting polarities of love, assertion, weakness, and strength—combined with a deep reliance on the Holy Spirit—support our transformation from the inside out.

The virtues of God's psychology embedded in the self compass include charity, good cheer, courage, creativity, empathy, objectivity, discipline, and autonomy.

Charles Stanley writes that

God's ultimate goal for man necessitates that his work be done in the Spirit. He is out to alter the heart of man, to bring about a renewal from the inside out. That cannot be done apart from the influence of the Holy Spirit. . . . When the Holy Spirit has been part of something, you will always find fruit, character, restored relationships, and men and women whose lives radiate the love of Jesus Christ.[1]

Each of the four compass points contributes two essential virtues to the whole of a healthy personality. Love contributes charity and good cheer. Assertion brings courage and creativity. Weakness offers empathy and objectivity. Strength provides discipline and autonomy (see fig. 11.1). The love of God at the center of the personality anchors the self compass.

A fully functioning self compass increases effective living and intimacy with God. The process of creating wholeness in the personality is a rhythm of making continuous growth stretches, assimilating lost parts of ourselves, surrendering to the power of healing prayer, and bonding with friends in a common quest for wholeness. Tools that can support our journey toward wholeness include the Word of God, church fellowship, small group ministries, pastoral counseling, psychotherapy, prayer, and the LAWS of God's psychology.

My personal and clinical experience suggests that people who have been deeply hurt are attracted to these LAWS the most. Once sufficient recovery has taken place, these individuals often develop an extraordinary capacity for wholeness precisely because they so keenly feel these virtues.

THE CHURCH IN THE TWENTY-FIRST CENTURY

Transformation toward Christlikeness is carried out one person at a time. Yet the principles of God's psychology apply to larger groups as well.

You see, groups take on the personality patterns of their leaders. When leaders grow toward health, a ripple effect sends out waves of change throughout the group.

As we saw in the case of Fran, a departmental head in her corporation, the more whole her personality became, the more her entire department shifted from authoritarian control to democratic self-expression. The group personality itself was altered. Esprit de corps, transparency, and caring prevailed, giving the group new life and freedom.

The body of Christ can grow toward wholeness only one person at a time. The purification of personality can't be legislated or

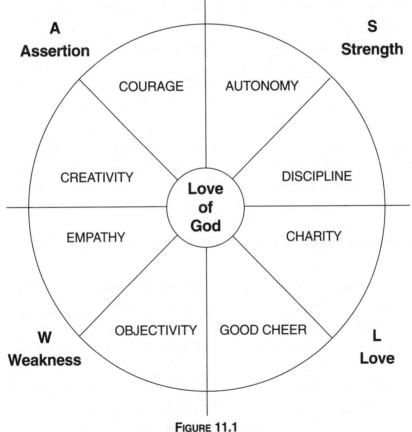

FIGURE 11.1
THE VIRTUES OF THE SELF COMPASS

forced on anyone. In the twenty-first century, I foresee grassroots changes in the way local churches meet the needs of their congregations.

The principles of God's psychology are already catching on in churches around the world. If the Holy Spirit so directs, this movement has real potential for the transformation of individual Christians and their local churches.

Let me share my personal vision for the role of the church in the twenty-first century. I foresee a worldwide movement among churches that emphasizes the principles of God's psychology. Pastors will be equipped with adequate training in life-span psychology and therapeutic counseling. Licensed Christian counselors will serve congregations on the church premises. Small group ministries will abound, favoring a dynamic model of personal encounter, confession, and prayer. Pastors will preach about the connection between spirituality and personality growth.

Support services will include marriage enrichment, child-rearing education, and day care facilities for families. Small group ministries will build a warm interpersonal climate within the church. Programs and activities for young people will minister to the developmental needs of that age group. Boys and girls will learn how to develop a whole self compass.

These ministries and services will glorify Christ as He purifies personalities and relationships.

The church of the twenty-first century will attract people from diverse backgrounds and ethnic groups by being accepting. From a healthy position of maturity, Christianity will renew its call to those who previously rejected Christ because of rigidities and biases within churches.

The Father, Son, and Holy Spirit will be free to do what they do best: "Bring good news to the suffering and afflicted . . . comfort the broken-hearted . . . announce liberty to captives and . . . open the eyes of the blind" (Isa. 61:1 TLB).

THE GROUP PERSONALITY OF THE LOCAL CHURCH

In addition to personality transformation in individual Christians, the twenty-first century will witness the group personality of local churches growing toward greater psychological and spiritual wholeness. A church often patterns itself after its elders, board, and pastor. But with more Christians making the change from rigid personalities to the principles of God's psychology, there will be greater health in Christian leadership. Churches formerly hindered by defeating partial trends can mature into Christlike congregations.

- Dependent churches, which lack a backbone, can learn to express stronger identities through greater assertion.

- Histrionic churches, which are overly enthusiastic and make much ado about nothing, can temper their whoop-de-do with more substance.

- Paranoid churches, which are suspicious of outsiders and divisive to the body of Christ, can mellow out and find needed health through more love and humility.

- Antisocial churches, which exploit people as "things" to meet the needs of a few, can learn how to serve and heal whole congregations.

- Avoidant churches, where Christians are overly shy and retiring, can grow into churches with confidence in the power of the Holy Spirit.

- Schizoid churches, which are characterized by reclusive isolation, can come alive and get involved in their local communities.

- Compulsive churches, where people are obsessed with the hobbyhorse of perfection and self-righteousness, can become more effective witnesses through a new compassion for the imperfect.

- Narcissistically driven national media ministries can learn to discipline themselves, encouraging their viewers to financially support their local churches.

My prayer is that by the grace of God, the twenty-first century will bring us closer to Christ than ever, as we submit ourselves to the Holy Spirit's purifying power within our personalities.

CHAPTER 12

Change in Your
Own Backyard

Be transformed.

—Romans 12:2

Danny Charles's mother stood a mere five feet tall, yet she seemed to him a Goliath. Ever since he could remember, she was pushing him forward into the world of people, never mind how shy and introverted he felt.

He recalled a scene from childhood:

Mother dragged me by the wrist downtown to the shoe store. I was about ten years old. "Mr. Hoffman," she told the owner of the store in a high-pitched voice, "get five pairs of shoes out here right this minute. Danny needs a new pair for his birthday party. Do you have any colors other than black? Black is so dull!"

Mr. Hoffman hopped like a rabbit back and forth, opening so many pairs of shoes it looked like Christmas—empty boxes and tissue everywhere. Other people came into the store, but they had to wait.

"There's the perfect pair," she exclaimed, pointing to a red pair of tie-up shoes. I cringed. I'd be the laughingstock of my school.

"Don't you just love them?" she asked without waiting for my reply. "Wrap them up, Mr. Hoffman. Danny loves them!"

This man had many such vivid memories.

Danny Charles's mother handled his adult life with antagonism and smothering nosiness. She opposed his vocation, took a strong stand against his marriage, and expressed views contrary to whatever he believed. In his thirties, he thought, *I don't know who I am. My mother dominates my thoughts, feelings, and actions. God, help me!*

Danny Charles applied principles of God's psychology and prayer to heal his personality. He took growth stretches into assertion and strength to find the courage to cut the psychological umbilical cord to his mother. He wanted Christ to be the center of his life.

He flourished in his new growth, experiencing the joy of intimacy, identity, and community with others. Danny Charles finally made his declaration of independence from his mother. He got her moodiness, criticisms, and negativity out from inside him. For the first time, he lived life with freedom and joy, trusting the Holy Spirit to guide him daily.

Then the strangest thing happened. He felt God calling him to return to his mother and help her. "No way!" he said to the still, small voice. "I can't stand to have anything to do with Mom ever again!" But over months, the gentle voice prevailed.

Danny, the voice explained, *I've set you free to be your real self. You've learned how to stand on your own feet, handle vulnerability, express yourself, and love others. Now it's time to love your mother.*

Reluctantly, Danny Charles made arrangements to spend several months living with his mother. She was eighty years old. Her husband had passed away. She lived alone.

Their first months together were stormy. His mother wasn't about to hear from her son what she had avoided hearing for a lifetime. He tried delicately to help her see that her aggression and constant negativity drove people away. She would explode into tirades that lasted for hours.

The fourth month, Danny Charles had a reckoning with God. "Dear Lord, You sent me here to help Mom, but she's only getting worse. I'm going crazy. I'll stay one more week."

A few days later Danny Charles and his mother took a short trip together. In the middle of the drive, the inner voice of the Lord prompted Danny Charles to go for broke. He took a breath and started speaking softly, but firmly:

"Mom, I've got to say a few things and I'd appreciate it if you'd just listen." He saw her set her jaw, stiffen her neck, and glare straight ahead.

"You were raised as a child piano prodigy and had your own radio show by the age of twelve. By thirteen you played for two civic clubs in town. You were the most colorful and talented of your ten brothers and sisters. Everybody thought you were the center of the universe—including you. What happened is that all your childhood confidence made you a sassy know-it-all. As an adult and a parent, you believed that the world was at your command.

"To get your way you threw temper tantrums, screamed a lot, made ugly faces, and harangued for hours. But to the townspeople you put on smiles and played the piano with a passion. I've been trying to have a two-way conversation with you my whole life, but it's been impossible. You butt in, jump to conclusions, get defensive, become nervous, and do everything in your power to keep from hearing the truth about your behavior.

"Mom, I want to say there's a better way. For whatever years you have left, you can choose to become a positive, sensitive, and caring woman who uses humor and affection instead of aggression and hostility. I love you, Mom, but I know that if you don't change soon, you'll die without ever having a single decent conversation with your son."

His mother sat in silence for the next ten minutes. Then she spoke in a quiet voice: "Danny Charles, every word you've said is true. I've never understood my life until just now. God has spoken to me through you."

Over the next year Anna changed so noticeably that all the family members could talk of little else. There was a humility in her, an ability to share the limelight with others and listen while others spoke. Her old arrogance shifted into quiet confidence. Her aggression all but disappeared, bringing good cheer and a wonderful ability to bolster the spirits of others. Her self-absorption was transformed into tender caring. Whether through phone calls, greeting cards, or personal visits, Anna could be counted on to say a hearty, "I love you! May the joy of the Lord be with you!"

The story of Danny Charles and his mother, Anna, shows how anyone can change—even in fundamental ways. There is beauty in every stone. By accepting God's grace and applying the wisdom of God's psychology, people can find their way to health and happiness—right in their own backyard.

I know. I'm Danny Charles.

PART 4

Globe of Human Nature

Now may the God of peace Himself sanctify you completely; and may your whole spirit, soul, and body be preserved blameless at the coming of our Lord Jesus Christ.

—Paul

1 Thessalonians 5:23

CHAPTER 13

Your Human Nature

This also we pray, that you may be made complete.

—2 Corinthians 13:9

Part 1 has shown you how to loosen the rigidity of your personality patterns with the help of the Lord. The principles of God's psychology covered so far have introduced you to these concepts.

There are four universal compass points of personality—love, assertion, weakness, and strength. Depending on your choices, these dynamic polarities are the source of stuckness or rhythmic integration within the self compass. Growth stretches allow you to transform rigid patterns of a partial personality into rhythmic swings of a healthy personality. You need God's ever-present love at the center of your being—guiding, comforting, and sculpting the process of your development.

But you need something else on the journey of wholeness. You need to understand and cooperate with your human nature, which God has created. The second thrust of God's psychology goes deeper than your attitudes and behaviors right down to the level of your being.

God's psychology asserts that we are God-created beings with minds, hearts, bodies, and spirits. The continued enhancement of our personalities and relationships requires facing these dimensions of our natures and bringing them into working accord. Once

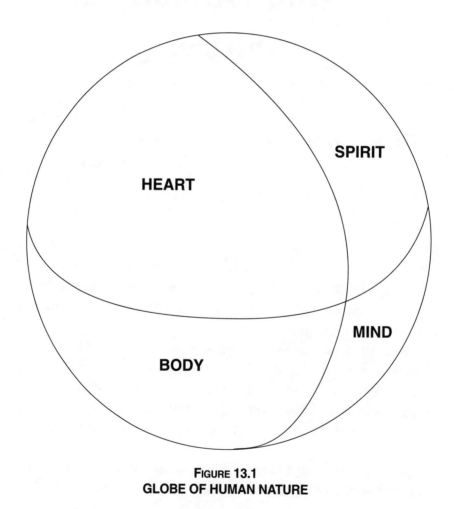

FIGURE 13.1
GLOBE OF HUMAN NATURE

*We need God because
we need an intelli-
gence greater than
our own to show us
the way through life,
a love greater than
our own to combat
our fears, and a per-
sonality more whole
than our own to heal
and comfort us.*

> *You need God's ever-present love at the center of your being— guiding, comforting, and sculpting the process of your development.*

again, we need God's help in developing our whole selves.

The globe of human nature symbolizes the need for mind, heart, body, and spirit to receive equal consideration and rhythmic integration for us to grow in Christ (see fig. 13.1).

Our *minds* need openness, discipline, and humility. Our *hearts* need friendship, trust, and intimacy. Our *bodies* need nutrition, exercise, and relaxation. Our *spirits* need salvation, renewal, and adventure. We need to awaken all four aspects of our natures and use them in dynamic rhythm with each other.

God created your human nature—mind, heart, body, and spirit—and wants to see you flourish. You need to take stock of each aspect, finding out which part is underdeveloped or which part is exaggerated. Part 2 shows you how to take growth stretches that correct your partially functioning nature, leading to the healthy human nature reflected in Christ.

Jesus came to affirm our human natures as He affirmed His own. He had a humble mind, an intimate heart, a vital body, and an adventurous spirit. The Son of God and the Son of man lived wholeheartedly without the hindrance of a partially functioning nature. And He says to us today, "My purpose is to give life in all its fullness" (John 10:10 TLB).

CHAPTER 14

A Humble Mind

Lean not on your own understanding.

—Proverbs 3:5

All who walk with the Lord are challenged to open their minds to His mysterious ways. Abraham opened his mind to God's strange promise, that his ninety-year-old wife, Sarah, would conceive a child. His humble mind allowed him to believe the impossible dream.

Moses shook in his sandals when he thought of confronting Pharaoh with God's demand to deliver the Jewish people out of Egypt. But through his ongoing dialogue with the Lord, Moses opened his mind to God's direct guidance. Moses' flexible thinking allowed him to obey God's unusual commands.

An angel appeared to Mary and announced that the Holy Spirit would

> *All who walk with the Lord are challenged to open their minds to His mysterious ways.*

—173—

mysteriously father the Son of God through her. The angel praised Mary for her humble and receptive mind.

After Christ's ascension into heaven, the apostle Peter made up his mind that only Jews could be saved. The Holy Spirit gave him an inspired dream that contradicted his rigid bias: "What God has cleansed you must not call common" (Acts 10:15). Peter opened his mind and responded to God's new directions. He preached the gospel in the Gentile household of Cornelius. After all gathered had received the Holy Spirit, Peter said, "In truth I perceive that God shows no partiality. But in every nation whoever fears Him and works righteousness is accepted by Him" (Acts 10:34–35).

Scripture refers to the importance of a humble mind in this way:

For as the heavens are higher than the earth,
So are My ways higher than your ways,
And My thoughts than your thoughts (Isa. 55:9).

NEW WINESKINS

Sometimes we think we've figured God out. We judge everyone according to what we think are God's standards. Occasionally, God has to dash our prideful thinking to pieces.

The eight partial personality patterns described in this book show eight different ways we can close our minds. Each pattern embodies a set of inflexible attitudes—a "hardening of the ough-teries." As long as they are intact, our thinking is intractable—we unknowingly resist the grand adventure of God's will.

Following the Lord on a daily basis requires a maximum openness so that we can keep revising our narrow assumptions into more complete versions of the truth. Remember Christ's metaphor about wineskins? The new wine of the Spirit-led life must continuously be put into fresh wineskins of new attitudes, perceptions, and values. Humble minds are constantly renewed, while rigid minds get stuck in a rut.

"Authentic Christian thought," writes Gabriel Marcel, "is an open thought *par excellence*. . . . A real orthodoxy creates those conditions rooted in the supernatural which unfold the most spacious and unbounded horizons for human knowledge and action."[1]

The more obedient to Christ's Spirit we become, the more our minds are humbled. We find that God's majesty and mystery cannot be contained within rigid mental perceptions. Our search for truth expands beyond vain traditions or self-serving righteousness. We are responsive to the genius of God in daily living. We surrender to the humble truth that "God has chosen the foolish things of the world to put to shame the wise, and God has chosen the weak things of the world to put to shame the things which are mighty" (1 Cor. 1:27). Giving up our rigid attitudes brings us liberty—a sense of creative living—in the Holy Spirit: "Where the Spirit of the Lord is, there is liberty" (2 Cor. 3:17).

THE UNFORCED RHYTHMS OF GRACE

How do we maintain a judicious rhythm between open-mindedness and self-control? How do we learn to experience a mental equilibrium in daily life? How do we enjoy the liberty of the Spirit without being blown about by every wind of doctrine or seduced by vain philosophy? "For God has not given us a spirit of fear, but of power and of love and of a sound mind" (2 Tim. 1:7).

We need to benefit from both liberty and structure. As we've seen, human nature is characterized by polarities. Healthy people have a rhythm of being loving yet assertive, weak yet strong, disciplined yet spontaneous. This rhythm exists within our personalities, and it is expressed through our relationships with others and God. We need to skate between these opposite poles as artfully as an ice-skater doing figure eights.

> *A sound mind requires humbly accepting the many complementary opposites that exist within us.*

Theologian Henri Nouwen writes, "To live a spiritual life means first of all to come to the awareness of the inner polarities between which we are held in tension."[2] A sound mind requires humbly accepting the many complementary opposites that exist within us.

Tolerating opposites within ourselves and others lets us say,

- I am sometimes strong and sometimes weak.
- I am sometimes loving and sometimes angry.
- I am sometimes spiritual and sometimes sinful.
- I am sometimes open and sometimes defensive.
- But God accepts, forgives, and loves me just as I am.
- And I can accept, forgive, and love myself and others.

God is always willing to forgive and accept us if we judge ourselves and surrender to His love.

THROUGH HUMILITY, WE ARE STRENGTHENED

What does it mean to judge ourselves so that we can surrender to God's love? We quit focusing on petty issues about right and wrong—swatting gnats but swallowing camels—and get to the root of the problem of sin, our faulty selves.

By admitting to our personality defects, we face the reality of sin in our lives. By confessing our wrongful thinking—our rigid patterns as clinging vines, prima donnas, bullies, con artists, wallflowers, hermits, big shots, and perfectionists—we are gradually healed: "If we confess our sins to him, he can be depended on to forgive us and to cleanse us from every wrong" (1 John 1:9 TLB).

We give up our excuses, pretenses, and self-righteousness, and we announce our guilt. We can't make it alone. Humbling our minds to God avails us of His help, one day at a time.

A liberating paradox is at work. If we humble our minds, we receive wisdom. If we declare our guilt openly, we are declared innocent. If we surrender our self-sufficiency, our lives become grace filled. By acknowledging our perpetual weaknesses, we are strengthened by the Holy Spirit.

And here lies the mysterious balance between structure and liberty: the nature of God is the Logos or Final Structure of His creation. Yet when we live within this structure, we have life, liberty, and love. Growing in the Lord means outgrowing religion for religion's sake and falling more deeply in love with Jesus, the living Word.

By humbling ourselves before the Lord and others, we tap into His eternally generous nature. His personal love for us leads to spontaneity, intimacy, and adventure. We experience the joy of the Lord, yet live within His discipline. We follow His commandments, and they bless us. We seek to do His will, and He fulfills the desires of our hearts.

Jesus captured the graceful interplay between structure and liberty, discipline and spontaneity, when He taught us to pray,

Our Father in heaven,
Reveal who you are.
Set the world right;
Do what's best—
    as above, so below.
Keep us alive with three square meals.
Keep us forgiven with you and forgiving others.
Keep us safe from ourselves and the Devil.
You're in charge!

You can do anything you want!
You're ablaze in beauty!
    Yes. Yes. Yes.[3]

THE RHYTHM OF REASON
AND FAITH

During my junior year of college, my philosophy professor—a brilliant woman—called me to her office one afternoon. The warmth of the room was a welcome contrast to the biting cold of the New Mexican winter.

I sat down and waited for Dr. Gibbens to speak. She handed me an essay I'd written. Across the top, she'd printed *SPLENDID!*

Tilting back in her chair, she said, "Dan, I'd like to deepen your perspective on Western philosophy. I've made a list of books by Plato, Kant, Schopenhauer, Sartre, and some others. I wonder if you'd be willing to read them on your own."

I thought for a moment. "Dr. Gibbens, I have a deep faith in God. What if these philosophers get me on the wrong track?"

She smiled and folded her hands on the desk. "Dan, faith that is untested is simpleminded. You haven't really wrestled with the great questions. Until you do, you won't have much to offer the world."

"I can tell people that God loves them."

"If God is loving," she asked, "then why is there evil in the world? Why does He let little children die of cancer? Why doesn't He prevent earthquakes, famines, and wars?"

I didn't know how to answer.

"Read these," she said, handing me a slip of paper. "Converse with the great minds of history. Then come back and we'll talk."

I left Dr. Gibbens's office determined to read the books.

That semester I pored over Hume's *A Treatise of Human Nature,* Schopenhauer's *The World as Will and Idea,* Nietzsche's

Beyond Good and Evil, and Sartre's *Being and Nothingness,* often reading far into the night, my head swimming with disconcerting new concepts. These philosophers made impressive arguments that God doesn't exist. By the time I finished *Being and Nothingness,* a darkness encompassed me. The philosopher's portrait of a universe without a heart stirred up searing memories of my troubled adolescence.

Near the beginning of my senior year in high school in September 1963, I stumbled into a church service desperately seeking God. That day love filled my being. Simple faith in Christ changed my life.

Now a handful of philosophers were challenging my faith with the power of human reasoning. I set up an appointment with Dr. Gibbens. I asked for her perspective on human history and humankind's need for God.

Pacing back and forth in front of the bookshelves, she spoke for two hours, covering the developments in Western art, science, philosophy, and religion. Her conclusion was that progress was made through the human ability to think rationally, and that there was no need for God.

Then she asked me the question I had dreaded: "Now tell me, how has your reading in philosophy squared with your faith in a loving God?"

I felt ashamed and confused. I confessed that I'd practically reasoned my faith away. She looked concerned. Then she uncapped her fountain pen and scribbled a few lines on a piece of paper.

"Dan, you were very brave to face the philosophers who did not believe in God," she said. "Now, here's a list of philosophers who encountered Christ the way you did. What you need is a balance of faith and reason. Faith without reason is blind. Reason without faith lacks spirit. I can't put the two together. Maybe you can."

I looked down at the list. St. Augustine. Blaise Pascal. Gabriel Marcel. Soren Kierkegaard.

I left Dr. Gibbens's office depressed and discouraged. I had originally wanted to share my faith in God with my professor. She had asked me to put my faith to the test. I had reasoned faith away and, if anything, was becoming intellectually arrogant. Now she was encouraging me to humble my mind and find faith again! How could I learn to walk this tightrope between faith and reason?

I read the books on Dr. Gibbens's list during my senior year. It was good to know of Christian philosophers. Kierkegaard, for example, touched me with the idea that an individual must freely choose a relationship with God, but even he could not resurrect my floundering faith.

A week after graduation, an old friend, Raina, called and asked if I would meet her at church for the Sunday night service. I cringed. Yet for some reason I said, "Okay, I'll be there." I hung up, angry. I'd meant to say no!

Raina had been a rebel in high school. But when I told her about God's love and offered to pray for her, she had accepted it. Raina had become a gentle, sincere person.

I arrived at the church late and sat in the back pew. I was in a nasty mood. Raina was sitting up toward the front. She glanced over her shoulder and smiled.

The reverend gave a sermon that annoyed me further. Then at the end he asked, "Does anyone have any comments about my sermon?"

I stood up and said, "Yes, your message about God's love was simpleminded. Your reasoning was flawed. Your sermon was stupid!"

The congregation sat hushed and frozen. The preacher paled. Then he walked down the aisle and gave me a big hug. "You're right, son," he said. "I didn't spend enough time on that sermon. Please forgive me. But I do love you and so does God."

I was dumbfounded. He wasn't embarrassed by his simple faith. He had countered my arrogance with love, and I felt an odd feeling—respect.

I rushed out of the church. Raina came up behind me and touched me gently on the shoulder. If she was appalled by my outburst, she didn't show it. "I've been praying for you, Dan. I've heard about how you're struggling with your faith. I want you to know that God will always love you." As I drove away, a sense of hollowness welled up in me.

Over the next two weeks, I realized that I had walked away from God, not vice versa. *God never told me I can't use my mind,* I thought. *Maybe I can love Him and be a thinker, too.*

Gradually, I was drawn back to Raina's church. At the end of another Sunday night service, I walked up to the altar and knelt. Several people gathered to pray with me. Someone whispered, "God still loves you, Dan." It was Raina's voice. I sighed deeply. The knot in my stomach began to loosen.

Suddenly, the dam of reserve burst, releasing a flood of emotion and repentance. I sobbed as the poisons of pride passed out of me.

A month later I was driving to Santa Fe. As I approached Apache Canyon, my body began to tremble. A voice from within whispered, *Turn off here. Go see Dr. Gibbens.*

Dr. Gibbens lived up the canyon road. Her gate was unlocked, so I let myself in and knocked on the door of her home. A weak voice invited me in.

Dr. Gibbens lay on the sofa, a blanket tucked around her.

"Dan Montgomery," she said softly, "I was just thinking about you. Sit down. I've been sick for three days, trying to fend for myself. I was remembering how you always talked to God and was wishing I could do that."

"That's incredible, Helen." It was the first time I had called her by her first name. "God told me to come here."

"Really? I've never been able to experience God—my intellect holds me back. The Christian religion seems like a snobbish club that either makes people arrogant know-it-alls or turns them into mindless dolts."

"Christians have the same flaws as other people. My relationship is with Jesus. I fell in love with Him when He came into my heart at seventeen. I came back to Him last month. He's my best Friend."

"Can God be my Friend?" said Helen, her eyes slightly moist. "Will you speak to God for me?"

I leaned over and laid my hand on Helen's forehead. "Father, Helen is tired of trying to figure You out. Come into her heart, forgive any wrong she's done, and reveal how much You love her. In Jesus' name."

Helen lay for a few moments with her eyes closed, breathing deeply, her face serene. Then her eyes blinked open, and she wiped tears from her cheeks with the edge of the blanket.

"I feel peace all through me," she said.

I made her a sandwich, refilled her water glass, and helped her to a more comfortable position. Golden rays from the setting sun streamed through the picture windows. God's love filled the room.

Later as I pulled back onto the highway, I reflected on Helen's glowing smile and the Bible's gentle promise:

Those of steadfast mind you keep in peace—
in peace because they trust in you (Isa. 26:3 NRSV).

CHAPTER 15

An Intimate Heart

*Go after a life of love as if your life depended on it—
because it does.*

—1 Corinthians 14:1 MESSAGE

Do you sometimes feel tied in emotional knots? Do fears get trapped inside you? Have you ever fallen in love when it was unwise to do so? Or exploded with anger in a destructive way? Have you ever felt numbed by inexplicable depression?

Feelings are the messiest, yet most rewarding part of living. Emotions are the power of personality. Even so, many people are baffled about how to express them.

I know something about emotional confusion. When I was growing up, my family didn't handle emotions well. There was an undercurrent of emotional tension, but nobody talked about it. Dad never said much or showed his emotions. Mom gushed feelings like Niagara Falls—I felt overwhelmed by her.

I absorbed the unhealthy emotional patterns of my parents. I swung between the two extremes: shutting down my feelings like

Dad or having emotional outbursts like Mom. As an adult, I was concerned about my emotional ineptitude. Stuffing my feelings or blurting them out got me in trouble with people. I even went through the wringer with the Lord because I didn't know how to express my feelings to Him.

But during my journey of personal growth and counseling others, I discovered several principles about emotions. Over the past several years, I've made progress in understanding my feelings and expressing them diplomatically. My fear and confusion are largely gone. I feel good knowing that I can express my feelings to anyone. My intimacy with God and people has deepened.

INTIMACY IS A CHOICE

I've often told people at conferences that it's easier to get a college education or start a successful business than it is to build endearing and enduring bonds of intimacy with people and God. But if we don't pursue intimacy, we may not experience it at all.

> *If we don't pursue intimacy, we may not experience it at all.*

"I don't want to be intimate!" said a middle-aged pastor named Jack. He felt upset because his family described him as emotionally remote. "Why can't they be satisfied that I'm a moral person who never shirks my duty?" he asked me. "Why does my wife keep nagging me to share my feelings? Emotions bother me. I can live without intimacy. Don't I have a right to that choice?"

He hit the nail on the head. Emotional intimacy is a choice. And because many of us experience difficulty with feelings in general, and intimacy in particular, we close ourselves off from others. If we felt insecure in our early attempts at intimacy, we may have become wounded by cynicism. Was your heart pierced by the pain of love longed for, but not realized? How did your family of origin handle feelings of love and intimacy? Was there trust, encouragement, and warmth in your family? Or was there self-consciousness, discouragement, and fear?

When we've been emotionally wounded, we armor ourselves so as not to be hurt again. Jack had been wounded as a little boy. He never felt the joy of intimacy with his parents. Unknowingly, he reflected this same defensive pattern in his relationships with his wife and two sons.

One of Jack's sons launched a campaign of rebellious behavior—a misguided attempt to get his father's attention and love. But Jack responded by laying down the law in an unfeeling manner. His son rebelled more.

When I talked with Jack's wife, I found that she'd armored herself with the same remoteness as Jack. "If he's going to hide his feelings," she said, "then so am I. I've tried helping him be intimate for fifteen years. I've given up." I realized that this couple had already gone through with an emotional divorce.

In a later counseling session, I suggested to Jack that he had a God-given capacity for intimacy of the heart. I said that if he would face his inner resistances and fears, he could make progress in expressing all of his emotions. He could become a lover to his wife, a friend to his sons, and a soul mate to members of his congregation. Jack got angry.

"Dr. Montgomery, you've joined those who want me to change. But I have no intentions of changing." He ceased counseling.

Several months later Jack hit a new low. People in his church had complained to his bishop that they were tired of his insensitivity and lack of feelings. After much deliberation, the bishop asked Jack to resign from the church.

I empathize with Jack because I, too, went through years of being emotionally unavailable for intimacy. I didn't know how intimacy worked, so every feeble attempt I made backfired. I learned to hide behind my intellect and keep my emotional reserve. I couched my spiritual life in theological terms to defend against emotional vulnerability. But deep inside I knew I wasn't a loving person.

> *The intimacy of God's heart pursues us in search of a faithful response.*

Hiding our hearts would work if God hadn't placed love at the center of human existence. Love is a central aspect of God's character. The intimacy of God's heart pursues us in search of a faithful response. Many Christians are finally grasping that by learning how to handle their emotions, they are deepening their capacity to love God. As Jesus said, "You shall love the LORD your God with all your heart" (Matt. 22:37).

Scripture views the heart as the center of the inner being. So how can we make progress in unfurling our feelings and heeding the call of God? Key principles of emotional intimacy can help us respond to God and others with purer hearts.

I define *intimacy of the heart* as "a caring bond between two or more people who are learning transparent self-disclosure, mutual trust, how to 'take the elevator down,' the rhythm of restraint and expression, and how to modulate feelings."

TRANSPARENT SELF-DISCLOSURE

No one can make progress in emotional intimacy without conducting an honest exploration of past emotional bungling. Scripture makes it clear that God draws near to people with a contrite heart. *Contrite* means "repentant, humbled, open."

I recall when I first humbled my heart to God. I suddenly felt the weight of a life without God—the fact that my emotions were tied in knots and I couldn't clean up the mess. I realized that God wanted more from me than a well-defended heart.

At that moment, I could have resisted God and kept my bungled emotions, or I could have laid my heart on the line and asked God to cleanse it. Something welled up inside me—perhaps it was the grace of God flowing into my gaping need—and I chose intimacy of the heart over self-willed isolation.

That choice began a lifetime of seeking the Holy Spirit's counsel in cleansing my heart on a daily basis. Jesus prompted me again and again to disclose my real feelings to Him and others. I was afraid people wouldn't like the real me. In fact, for the longest time I didn't know who the real me was.

> *No one can make progress in emotional intimacy without conducting an honest exploration of past emotional bungling.*

But over the years I learned how to face my feelings of fear, guilt, need, anger, and love. My walk with God and others became more relaxed and intimate.

I call this process of emotional leveling *transparent self-disclosure.* Dr. Sidney Jourard suggests that people become in need of psychotherapy "because they have not disclosed themselves in some optimal degree to the people in their life."[1] The apostle James says it this way: "Admit your faults to one another and pray for each other so that you may be healed" (James 5:16 TLB).

How do we disclose ourselves to those around us? First, we shouldn't disclose ourselves indiscriminately. Jesus didn't. He shared certain insights and emotions with the public, but He reserved more private perceptions for the twelve disciples. Even among them He discriminated further, confiding His deepest feelings to Peter, James, and John. And among them, only John—the beloved disciple—was entrusted by Jesus with the care of His mother at the foot of the cross.

We need discriminating trust when selecting people with whom we will tell all. Many people have told me that they confided too much to the wrong person and later had the confidence betrayed. Some stopped trusting anyone with matters of the heart at that point.

I first risked sharing secrets of my heart with a college professor. I'd had a couple of classes with her. She seemed like an honest and caring person. I was about twenty years old at the time. I'd developed a more intimate relationship with God, but it was one of my first attempts to bare my soul to another human being.

I chose a time of day when no other students were around. The professor was about to leave her office. I asked if I could talk to her a while. She invited me in, smiled pleasantly, and asked how she could help me.

"I need to talk about my life," I said. "I don't know how to relate to people very well, and it bothers me. My relationships seem too superficial. I don't know how to deepen them."

"I've had that problem myself," she said. "Let's talk."

During the next hour, I found out how good it felt to pour out my heart to someone who respected my courage. But what amazed me even more was that this professor opened her heart to me. We both disclosed things we'd never told another human being. I left her office feeling the healing power of intimacy.

Lucky for me, I chose the right person, someone with sufficient maturity to reciprocate my transparent self-disclosure. Thus began a marvelous friendship that lasted for twenty years until she passed away.

I must point out, though, that there are no guarantees in building an intimate bond. That's why discernment is required. If we choose the wrong person or push too hard for intimacy that is not reciprocated, we can be hurt. It's realistic to assume that we will be hurt a number of times as part of our quest for intimacy.

We're not alone. Jesus was hurt, too, but He kept believing in those who believed in Him.

MUTUAL TRUST

Trust is shifting the basis of a relationship from a mere mental engagement to an experiential commitment. It is moving from the head to the heart. I use an exercise at conference workshops to demonstrate what I mean by trust.

I invite a volunteer to the front and then ask for two other people to stand behind her. Facing the volunteer, I say, "Do you trust that the people behind you will catch you if you lean backward?"

The person thinks for a moment and says, "Yes, I trust them."

I turn to the audience. "This volunteer is stating a thought that those behind her can be trusted. But this isn't the same as actually trusting them."

Facing the volunteer again, I say, "Go ahead and act out your trust. Allow yourself to fall backward."

At this moment, the volunteer always makes a weird face. She experiences doubt. She shifts from the head down to the heart. She probably thinks, *Will they really catch me?* Or *Will I fall?*

She can't know the outcome until she takes the risk. If she feels that they are really trustworthy, she commits herself and falls into their arms. Inevitably, when the volunteer lets go of her control and falls, she experiences delight in being caught and supported in the arms of those she trusted.

Trust occurs in a relationship when you disclose something vulnerable and another person handles it with care and confidentiality. Mutual trust evolves, in turn, as he or she trusts you with something equally vulnerable. You build trust by pacing the exchanges, ever deepening the level of mutual disclosure. If either of you is unwilling to go deeper, it's wise to back off and respect this unreadiness.

A relationship can be maintained at whatever level is comfortable to both parties. So what are the levels of intimacy possible between people?

TAKING THE ELEVATOR DOWN

I use the image of "taking the elevator down" to describe the choice points for reaching deeper levels of intimate trust in a relationship.

The intimacy elevator starts with the *facade level,* or level of public appearances. Here, people relate through social custom. Conversations are filled with small talk about the weather, sports, earthquakes, families, and the state of the world. This is a valuable and necessary stage for getting acquainted and for doing business with people we don't know well.

The next floor down is the *acquaintance level.* We reveal some of our private sentiments and opinions. At this level, we present more of our views on politics, religion, sex, and marriage. There is some risk that people will take offense. However, most people know how to participate in these exchanges without taking it personally.

To reach the third floor down, the *friendship level,* we must willingly experience emotional vulnerability. At this level, we share all sorts of feelings, yet hold back on the deeper ones. We look for compatibility, empathy, and mutual trust. If all goes well, and the other person responds at this same level, we may choose to take the elevator down another floor.

The fourth floor down is the *intimacy level.* We come clean with the dark side—the memories, wounds, and reflections that make us who we are, but that can feel shameful to disclose. We also share the heart's desires. People who cannot reach this level in friendships or marriage may need a pastoral counselor or therapist to help them.

THE RHYTHM OF RESTRAINT
AND EXPRESSION

If a feeling persists in a relationship that you care about, it's wiser to express it than to repress it. But to ensure that the other person is receptive to the feeling, you need to exercise consideration. A person feels shocked if you dump an intense feeling on him out of the blue. Keeping this in mind, you learn to warm up someone to your feelings, all the more so if you intend to express a powerful emotion.

Watch for a time when the other person is feeling relaxed. Strike up a conversation. Take your time and build rapport. Mention that there is something on your heart you need to share. Ask if this is a good time to talk. Now that you've received attention and permission, express your feeling and the circumstances surrounding it in a sincere, straightforward way. Most people appreciate this kind of emotional leveling, especially when they've been properly warmed up.

Once you've expressed yourself, relax, sit back, and listen to the person's response. Develop a rhythm of dialogue that lets both feel heard. Take to heart what the other is saying. Usually, emotional honesty clears the air of phoniness and restores trust in the relationship.

> *Emotional communication requires restraint as well as expression.*

Emotional communication requires restraint as well as expression. You can express most emotions, even anger, in a calm and clear manner. You don't need to turn up the volume of your feelings so loud that others are blown away.

Expressions at the fullest level of intensity usually cause hurt, confusion, and anger in others. If love isn't the underlying motivation for disclosing feelings, you end up like "sounding brass or a clanging cymbal" (1 Cor. 13:1). The bottom line is that feelings expressed at lower levels of intensity with a degree of diplomatic restraint are more likely to be accepted and understood by others.

HOW TO MODULATE FEELINGS

Modulation refers to a sensitive variation in intensity. A good orchestra conductor knows how to vary the intensity of the music from pianissimo to fortissimo and can gracefully bring about these modulations.

But people stuck in rigid personality patterns can't vary the intensity of their emotional expression. They're stuck on loud or soft. And they lack a full orchestra of emotions. Like playing a symphony without strings, brass, or woodwinds, people with rigid patterns exclude entire poles of expression.

Dependent clinging vines and histrionic prima donnas exclude assertion and strength. They never learn how to modulate emotions such as *annoyance, indignation, resentment,* and *anger.* These feelings get stuck inside them and deteriorate into the negative emotional baggage of bitterness, jealousy, petulance, and depression. People stuck on the love compass point can't achieve intimacy, for their efforts to be close to others degenerate into pleasing and placating.

What about paranoid bullies and antisocial con artists? These individuals have plugged up their capacity for love. They don't know how to modulate feelings of *fondness, affection, forgiveness,* and *compassion.* These feelings get stuck inside and collapse into cynicism, distrust, sadism, and hatred. People stuck on the assertion compass point are blocked from finding intimacy because their behavior is contaminated by abusing and exploiting.

Avoidant wallflowers and schizoid hermits have never come to terms with their fear of people. They avoid the risk taking that love requires, and they isolate themselves. They don't know how to modulate feelings from the strength compass point, such as *adequacy, confidence, determination,* and *courage.* These feelings decay into numbness, hopelessness, shame, and panic attacks. By remaining stuck on the weakness compass point, they have their needs for intimacy sabotaged by their detachment and withdrawal.

Nascissistic big shots and compulsive perfectionists are stuck on the strength compass point. They don't know how to modulate feelings of *uncertainty, anxiety, guilt,* and *helplessness.* They avoid these feelings by girding themselves with conceit, condescension, arrogance, and pomposity. By staying on the strength compass point, they make intimacy impossible because of their overbearing self-sufficiency.

Rhythmic Swings of Emotion

Even if we're stuck in self-defeating personality patterns, we long for love. We feel frustrated that intimacy eludes us, and sometimes we intensify our patterns instead of giving them up! But the Holy Spirit will help free us from patterns that block intimacy of the heart.

A woman wrote to me the other day: "Dear Dr. Dan, I am working on facing my real feelings. I seem to be stuck in my anger. Last night in prayer the Lord seemed to say, 'Do you want to be healed?' I am finding myself finally wanting to be healed more than wanting to hang on to the anger and pain."

To gain insights into your emotional pattern, watch how you modulate the emotions of each compass point for one week. Draw four columns on a sheet of paper. Using one column for each of the four points—love, assertion, weakness, and strength—identify the feelings that you experience each day. Track the frequency with which certain feelings occur.

At the end of the week, tally the columns and see what you discover. Is one of the compass points exaggerated at the expense of the others? Ask yourself why you're not using your whole self compass. Then practice new growth stretches of emotional expression in the neglected compass points.

By modulating emotions of love and assertion, weakness and strength, you develop a range and rhythm of emotional response. You increase your interpersonal sensitivity.

Intimacy requires this full orchestration of human emotions. By your being your love and assertion, your weakness and strength with another person and with God, your spiritual essence blossoms. The love of God at the center of your being guides your emotional life and self-expression. The heart of Christ beats in you.

Paul prays that our "hearts may be encouraged, being knit together in love, and attaining to all riches of the full assurance of understanding, to the knowledge of the mystery of God, both of the Father and of Christ, in whom are hidden all the treasures of wisdom and knowledge" (Col. 2:2–3).

With patience and practice, we will develop intimacy of the heart and receive treasures from the heart of Jesus Christ.

INTIMACY WITH GOD

How do we avail ourselves of the full power of the Holy Spirit in our everyday lives if we often feel remote from God? When we pray, do our prayers sometimes fall from the ceiling like lead balloons? We long to feel close to God, but we can't break out of the blues. Our discouragement increases. Faith decreases. We wonder if God can handle our real feelings.

Last year the Holy Spirit spoke to my wife, Katie, and me on the way home from dinner at a restaurant. The presence of God was so palpable in the car that I pulled over to the side of the road, where we prayed. We both received a clear impression that Katie was to leave her twenty-year college career and become my full-time editor.

We talked this over during the week, and we received additional confirmations that it was the will of God. So we took a leap of faith, and Katie resigned. Over the next year we wrote together. Predictably, our finances took a nosedive. Soon we were living on one-half our former incomes. "How are we going to make it?" I wondered. From time to time, powerful feelings of anxiety, depression, annoyance, and panic streamed through me.

I have to admit—my prayer life felt like a roller coaster ride! Each time I talked to God, I'd run the gamut of emotions. I struggled with how honest my prayers should be. Could God handle my panic about finances and my frustration over no manuscript sales? Katie feared that we were disappointing God with our lack of perfect faith.

Behind the scenes, however, Katie's able assistance was increasing my productivity remarkably. Normally, it takes me about a year to write a book. With Katie's help, I finished three books by year's end. But we'd exhausted our savings, and we hadn't signed any contracts.

We mulled over how we could remain intimate with God in a time of great stress. Gradually, we came to the conclusion that prayer is not only about loving God but also about leveling with Him. We reasoned that our heavenly Father is wise and omniscient, and He sees into our hearts at all times. The point of intimacy with God isn't to inform Him about what He already knows but to strengthen our trust in Him.

Emotional honesty with God helps us know how much He loves us. Whether we cry out with fear or dance with joy, He is with us, tenderly guiding. I remember nights in my bedroom that year when I'd praise God with arms raised high and laughter in my soul. Other nights, though, I'd pace back and forth, ranting and raving about how we were up a creek without a paddle.

> *Emotional honesty with God helps us know how much He loves us.*

Katie shut down her feelings at first, fearful that God would judge her as lacking in faith. We talked this over, and she gradually grew as animated in talking with God as she is with me. Some nights her face showed dejection, and other nights, pure joy.

Not to worry. God delights when we trust Him to handle our real feelings. Often peace comes in the wake of honest, intimate prayer. We know that God is with and for us, one day at a time.

You can imagine how we jumped for joy the week we received word that all three of our manuscripts had been accepted for publication! We literally stood in the center of the living room with our hands locked together, and we danced around and around for joy.

When we open our hearts to the wisdom of God's psychology, the Holy Spirit cleanses us of our negativity and rejoices with us in our triumphs. We find that God is in the intimate details of daily life.

CHAPTER 16

A Vital Body

Glorify God in your body.
—1 Corinthians 6:20

After graduation from university with my bachelor's degree, I was preparing for my second stint as a summer stock actor for the Kaleidoscope Players, a theater company.

While I was packing my suitcase, a distinct inner prompting came to my heart: *Dan, I don't want you to take this theater job. I want you to be a children's counselor this summer. You'll be contacted shortly. If you wish to follow Me, accept the position that will be offered to you.*

The directness of the message perplexed me. *Is this the Lord,* I wondered, *or is it my imagination?* I responded by praying that if the message was truly from God, I would obey it. But I needed confirmation: number one because I enjoyed the theater, and number two because I hated kids! I momentarily put the message out of my mind and continued packing. A few minutes later the message came more forcefully.

I awoke the next morning willing to change my plans if someone contacted me about counseling children. During breakfast, the telephone rang. It was my brother-in-law calling me from his summer camp for kids—Western Life Camp. The camp is nestled in the Sangre de Cristo Mountains in northern New Mexico.

"Dan," he said, "I've run into a major snag. A guy from New York was going to be the junior boys' counselor. He just canceled out on me. Camp starts Friday. Can you take the position? You'll have to show up tomorrow."

I hesitated for a moment, remembering how much I disliked children. While I paused, a shiver of excitement pulsed through my body. I sensed that this must be the Holy Spirit giving me a green light.

"Dan," Mel asked, "are you still there?"

"Yes," I said, "I'm here. And yes, I'll see you at the camp tomorrow." When I hung up, a peace settled over me, a calmness that often comes when I find myself in God's will.

The next morning, I called the theater director and asked if my contract could be canceled on such short notice. Fortunately, the gracious man said that an understudy could take my place. That afternoon I made the drive up the winding mountain road to the camp. Pines and piñons dotted the canyon walls. Down below about a half mile, I could see the glimmering reflection of the Gallinas River.

Rounding a bend, I turned left and pulled into Western Life. There was a semicircle of log cabins, including a mess hall and recreation building, as well as a half-dozen smaller cabins for campers. In the middle of the camp lay an acre of grass-filled meadow, edged on the north side by the Gallinas River.

Mel greeted me warmly and temporarily assigned me to a cabin with four other counselors in their early twenties. He explained that we'd have two days for orientation. The ninety-odd campers would swoop down on us on Friday.

That night, I read the Bible until lights out. After a couple of doubt-filled years in college, I was reorganizing my life around Christ, and I needed all the help I could get. Quietness settled over the whole camp. I lay in the dark with my eyes open, hearing the rhythmic breathing of the four other guys who were sound asleep.

I wondered how I could cope with ten junior boys, since I'd always felt so impatient around children. Without warning, a point of light appeared in the center of the cabin. I thought it might be a reflection from something, but it expanded into rays of white light within a circle of radiance. The light was utterly brilliant, yet didn't hurt my eyes. My heart caught as I held my breath.

I could see nothing but millions of sparkling beams emanating from a compact center point. Slowly, the center of the light approached until it touched me. Sensations of pure love streamed into my body, permeating my deepest being. I felt cradled and hugged by God the Father. I felt no fear. As the Bible says, "Perfect love casts out fear" (1 John 4:18).

The divine hug intensified. The Lord spoke in the depths of my being: *Dan, you are My beloved son.* Joy cascaded through my body. In that moment I felt completely accepted and understood!

The rapture became so strong I couldn't contain it. I cried out silently, "No more!" I feared that I'd start dancing or laughing and making a fool out of myself. A microsecond later, the tender presence eased back.

The light that flooded the room gradually receded into the original center point and then vanished. I lay there in the pitch dark, taking in that God really is our Father.

The other guys were still sleeping soundly. No one else was roused by the light. I got up, dressed, and slipped out the door into the star-spangled night. I looked up and saw the Big Dipper. A pleasant afterglow pulsed in my body. Led by moonbeams, I followed a trail away from the camp and up to the rifle range, well out of earshot. There, I raised my arms to the heavens and yelled with all my might, "I love You, too!"

It still remains a mystery as to why and how this happened. But the next day, I got up feeling an incredible love for the kids who were coming to camp. I played and laughed with them all summer. Many of my old inhibitions—including a dislike of children and an unwillingness to hug—vanished with the touch of God's love that night.

A SIMPLE TOUCH

One of my friends, Mac, has worked for more than twenty years as a clinical chaplain in a state hospital. I asked him how he managed to communicate with developmentally disabled children.

"I touch them a lot," Mac answered, his eyes beaming. "Words don't mean much to them. If I just talked, they wouldn't understand me. But I've learned to communicate with my body. I touch them with my hands, caress them with my voice, and wink at them with my eyes—and they feel accepted. If I really didn't love them, they'd be the first to know it. They read the language of the body and can sense the presence or absence of love."

LOVE WITH SKIN ON IT

I've heard Jesus referred to as "Love with skin on." I like that. It shows how the Father's love flowed freely through Jesus' body and feelings into the lives of others. He often healed people by touching them. He expressed His emotions openly, and He welcomed the little children who wanted to touch Him.

Christ's compassion for people flowed through His hands, legs, arms, eyes, and face. Love flowed through His body. John says that not only did the disciples see the grace and glory of Jesus, but "our hands have *handled*" Him (1 John 1:1, italics mine). Paul states that in Jesus "dwells all the fullness of the Godhead *bodily*" (Col. 2:9, italics mine). Jesus manifested the power of His divinity in a physical way.

Physiological psychologist Howard Bartley wrote, "The person who gets great enjoyment out of his senses—that is, gets pleasure out of the sheer sensuous impact of his surroundings—is in pretty good mental health."[1] Jesus was such a person. He enjoyed His senses without being ruled by them. He also knew that touching can convey tender caring far better than words alone.

THE LAYING ON OF HANDS

Do you love your body and sense the presence of God in it? Some people have told me that the body is simply a machine that carries the head from place to place. But Paul asks, "Haven't you yet learned that your body is the home of the Holy Spirit God gave you, and that he lives within you?" (1 Cor. 6:19 TLB).

Bodies are specially created vessels through which God's love is meant to pour. In God's psychology, the works of Christ flow through our bodies.

Years ago, I was a psychology professor and counselor in a Christian liberal arts college. One Saturday while I was driving to a tennis court to volley with a friend, the Spirit of the Lord came upon me. I parked and prayerfully listened. The Lord asked me a strange question: *Dan, are you willing to give Me your eyes to see, your mouth to speak, your hands to touch, and your heart to love?*

I'd never before thought of God's desiring to use my body. While I pondered the question, it struck me that when Jesus walked the earth, He gave His entire body to the Father's will. The power of the Holy Spirit moved through His eyes, hands, and heart so that He could mirror the extravagant love of the Father.

Is the Father wanting me to make my body available to Him like Jesus did? I wondered. Talk about getting personal. I grasped that the Father, Son, and Holy Spirit wished to live through my entire nature.

"Yes, Lord," I said, "I'll try to give You my eyes, mouth, hands, and heart."

The following week I took a first step. When several students asked if I would pray for them, I did so—with their approval—by the laying on of hands. They reported afterward that our prayer felt comforting when the forehead and shoulder were gently touched.

Grace Stuart explains in a passage from *Narcissus:*

> It is too seldom mentioned that the baby, being quite small for quite a long time, is a handled creature, handled and held. The touch of hands on the body is one of the first and last of physical experiences and we deeply need that it be tender. We want to touch . . . and a culture that has placed a taboo on tenderness leaves us stroking our dogs and cats when we may not stroke each other. We want to be touched. . . . We are starved for the laying on of hands.[2]

Before the Lord asked if He could use my body, I had felt split between my role as a psychologist and my ministry as a Christian. But afterward, my counseling became infused with a constant spirit of prayer. My mind, body, and spirit acted in greater accord.

I began using more role-playing and stress reduction techniques in counseling. When the body is able to discharge years of pent-up muscle tension, people feel more alive and well. They also feel closer to God.

In compass counseling I've developed a repertoire of mind-heart-body approaches to the personality, often combining them with prayer. Working with the whole person is more effective than using verbal therapy alone.

As I learned to trust the Holy Spirit in my body, I noticed that I relaxed more in teaching, counseling, and speaking. I felt less in a professional role and more of a personal connection to God and people. After a day's work, I'd feel less tension and fatigue. Over time the knots in my shoulders, strain in my vocal cords, and tension headaches disappeared.

Including my body in my spiritual life enriches my family relationships. If my wife has a bad day, she doesn't need me to try to fix things with my analysis of the situation. She benefits most when I listen quietly while I hold her hand and comfort her in my arms later at night. If my daughter's high school team loses a softball game, she doesn't need a lecture on keeping her head up. A soft look and a supportive hug work wonders.

WHAT ABOUT DEPRESSION?

Most of us experience normal ups and downs in any given day. We get a raise, and we feel up. Later that day, we get a bill from the orthodontist for $1,000, and we feel down. A prayer is answered, and we feel up. We argue with a friend, and we feel down. Sporadic sadness coexists in a figure-eight rhythm with peace and contentment. Even Jesus experienced this rhythm.

But if our minds are foggy and our bodies fatigued most of the time, depression has become a way of life. The body is signaling that something is out of whack when it's all we can do to get out of bed in the morning. Chronic depression obstructs our awareness of God's presence.

Does feeling depressed mean we're not good Christians? No. We don't have to wear perpetual smiles or have perfect faith. Christ accepts us, foibles and all. He understands our rhythms of faith and discouragement, joy and sadness, high spirits and fatigue, because He, too, experienced these things.

Feeling depressed doesn't mean that we're not saved or being guided by God. Yet when depression persists, we need to face it and pray for understanding about what is causing it. With improved discernment, we can

> *Feeling depressed doesn't mean that we're not saved or being guided by God.*

alleviate depression without falling prey to the notion that we must be happy all the time.

We can recognize and do something about four forms of depression: depression from grief, biological depression, depression from overload, and depression from lost spiritual purpose.

Depression from Grief

A frequent cause of depression is the grief that hits us when we lose something that is precious or seems essential to life. A job. Financial security. Personal health. A home. A loved one.

Jeanette came to me with a broken heart. At thirty years old she had become a widow overnight. Her husband was killed in a car accident while returning from a trip. After listening to her dark agony, I suggested that she clear her calendar as much as possible over the next month. After a severe loss, the mind blurs, the muscles clench, and the spirit laments.

Many people overlook the first essential step in recovery: giving the body adequate rest for renewal and rebuilding the immune system. A mild shock can require several days of recuperation. A devastating shock such as Jeanette experienced can require one to three months for the body to regain its resiliency. So I encouraged Jeanette to take naps, do a minimum amount of work, and ask her sister for help with the children.

Three months later Jeanette was over the worst of her depression. It took the rest of the year for her to find equanimity of body and soul.

Christians need to realize that feelings of grief, emptiness, and sadness are part and parcel of living. Even Jesus felt depressed from time to time. He was "exceedingly sorrowful" (Matt. 26:38). He "groaned in the spirit" (John 11:33). He "grieved" (Mark 3:5). He was "troubled" (John 12:27). And He "wept" (John 11:35).

Christ had the courage to feel occasional discouragement while at the same time trusting Himself to the Father's care—just as we

The process of creating wholeness in the personality is a rhythm of making continuous growth stretches, assimilating lost parts of ourselves, surrendering to the power of healing prayer, and bonding with friends.

must do. As the psalmist said, "Weeping may endure for a night, but joy comes in the morning" (Ps. 30:5).

Biological Depression

A second kind of depression is not contingent on life events. Some people have inherited a biochemical imbalance that causes depression. Biological depression results when the body doesn't produce enough catecholamine molecules for the nervous system.

These molecules work directly to transmit bioelectrical impulses between billions of nerve cells. How does that affect how we feel? If there is a shortage of catecholamines, our thinking gets muddled, we feel down, and our bodies are easily fatigued. There isn't enough power to fire up the nervous system to a normal level of operation, let alone cope with daily stress.

What are the symptoms of biological depression? Ten clinical signs reveal the condition:

1. Loss of pleasure in activities that normally bring happiness.

2. A haunting fatigue that isn't relieved by sleep.

3. Erratic sleeping patterns such as insomnia, fitful sleeping, or early morning wakening.

4. Reduced sexual activity.

5. Decreased love and affection to the point of feeling indifferent toward friends and family members who are normally close.

6. Indecisiveness about even the simplest matters, accompanied by guilt over on-again, off-again handling of commitments.

7. Remorse and rumination about real or imagined shortcomings in the past.

8. Anxiety in the form of tension, fear, or irritability.

9. Vague and unpleasant sensations in the chest, stomach, and/or solar plexus causing an ominous "dark" or "blue" feeling.

10. Suicidal thoughts that grow into vivid fantasies and deliberate planning.

The persistence of several of these symptoms over a period of months or years is the strongest indicator of biological depression. An appropriate antidepressant—which can be prescribed by a physician or psychiatrist—is a godsend.

Antidepressants provide the body with the needed neurotransmitters to bring the brain and nervous system up to par. The dark mood lifts, and a person becomes free to think more clearly, feel more vividly, and relax more easily.

If you're nearsighted or farsighted, you need glasses. If you're diabetic, you need insulin. And if you suffer from major depression, you may benefit from an antidepressant. Antidepressants are nonaddictive, antistress agents that—when properly prescribed—enhance the quality of health and happiness.

It is important not to judge biochemical depression as a moral lapse of faith or a negative attitude about life. People who receive the antidepressant that the body needs report within one to three weeks improved energy and mood stability. Sometimes, for the first time in their lives, they realize what it means to feel happy.

Depression from Overload

The overstimulation of modern life can cause a third type of depression. A mother scurries wearily from taxiing her children to cleaning the house, buying groceries, feeding the family, and working full-time outside the home. A worker is pushed to the limit by a compulsive boss or company. A job runs against the grain of personal ethics. Day after day we wake up to deadlines, endless bills, commuting, phone calls, urgent mail, depressing newscasts, and family needs.

How do we cope with the overstimulation of modern life? Instinctively, we tense our bodies, stuff our feelings, and numb our minds. We try to survive another day. By adapting to the pressure of constant crisis, we lose the serenity of spiritual and bodily grace.

We get used to living in a body that protests its neglect through such ailments as hypertension, fluctuating blood pressure, temporomandibular joint (TMJ) syndrome, headaches and stomachaches, ulcers, heart problems, or a host of vague complaints that even the doctor can't nail down.

It becomes tempting to get a warm glow or a momentary sense of relief from the following:

- Overeating
- Overdrinking
- Overexercising
- Oversleeping
- Hyping up with nicotine or coffee
- Calming down with tranquilizers

I've been guilty of most of these, especially during the years when I was more hard driving. But these are false remedies that end up abusing rather than helping the body. A downward spiral of depression increases as the body is weakened.

> *A daily surrender of my whole self to God is the only path to serenity in a pull-and-tug world.*

It wasn't until my midforties that I finally grasped the wisdom of God's psychology—that a daily surrender of my *whole* self to God is the only path to serenity in a pull-and-tug world.

Depression from Lost Spiritual Purpose

And the fourth cause of depression? When we're off track in discerning God's will and spiritual purpose for our lives. Scripture provides ample testimony that only God can fill the human mind, heart, body, and spirit with peace and love.

Fame and fortune, health and wealth, drugs and alcohol, or good intentions and hard work all fall short of fulfilling us as human beings. We need the Holy Spirit, not superficial substitutes, to dwell within us.

Sometimes depression can tip us off that we're living superficially, that we're not being true to ourselves, or that we're thwarting our Creator's plans for us. We may have to get real with God—confess, repent, and commit—before God can bless us.

Only as we surrender the control of our lives to God can the spiritual zest of the Holy Spirit fill our bodies. Western civilization is built on the premise that we should take responsibility and exercise control over our lives. But this contradicts Christ's teaching to seek first the kingdom of God and His righteousness, and trust God to provide for our daily needs. How do we escape this contradiction?

Again, the idea of a creative rhythm comes to our aid. We do need to take action for getting an education, acquiring a job, and—if we marry—raising our children. Think of this as taking hold of life. But that is not the last word. The rest of the creative rhythm that Christ speaks of involves letting go of life—trusting the Father for every need and concern, and calling on Him daily because He cares for us.

One woman had exchanged years of worry about controlling her life for a simpler trust in Christ. She told me, "My serenity is inversely proportional to my expectations. Acceptance is the key to my relationship with God. I do whatever is in front of me to be done, and I leave the results up to Him. However it turns out, that's God's will for me."

The rhythm of taking hold and letting go keeps us on a steady course of seeking God's unfolding will while doing our part daily to follow it. The Holy Spirit bears witness that dependence on God for everything is the pathway to hope. When we allow the whole nature to be sculpted by the Master's hands, beauty emerges from the stone. In the words of the psalmist: "My heart and my flesh cry out for the living God" (Ps. 84:2).

Yes, times of depression are normal for Christians. The good news is that major depression can be remedied through appropriate spiritual, therapeutic, or medical means—while milder depression prompts us to develop courage, patience, and trust in the Lord.

God wants to move through us without the interference of numbed or stressed-out bodies. As we loosen up and trust the Holy Spirit in our bodies, He can move upon us anytime and anywhere.

CHAPTER 17

An Adventurous Spirit

Behold, I will do a new thing.

—Isaiah 43:19

I believe that the Christian life is an adventure. I've felt this way ever since Jesus entered my heart at the age of seventeen. An adventure is an undertaking that involves risk and requires boldness. We can't experience adventure by sitting safely on the sidelines. An adventurous spirit incorporates our entire natures—mind, heart, and body—into our walk with God.

Heroes of faith such as Abraham, Moses, Mary, and Christ's disciples put everything on the line to follow God's will. Their faith was strengthened through the trials they endured. They risked persecution and hardship to engage wholly in their love affair with God. They were rewarded with destinies of grand adventure.

What can block our adventure in Christ? Anything that diminishes our love for the Father, Son, and Holy Spirit can lead us astray. Jesus said it this way: "He who loves father or mother more than Me is not worthy of Me. And he who loves son or daughter more than Me is not worthy of Me. And he who does not take his cross and follow after Me is not worthy of Me" (Matt. 10:37–38).

Our adventure in Christ is hindered if we put people or things before God. God alone is worthy of our complete trust. God alone can work out our heart's desires. He is a genius at guiding us to fulfillment within His overall plans. He helps us find life's meaning in remarkable ways. The more we surrender in love to God, the more He affirms our uniqueness and completes our destiny.

Jesus assures us:

> There is no one who has left house or brothers or sisters or father or mother or wife or children or lands, for My sake and the gospel's, who shall not receive a hundredfold now in this time . . . with persecutions—and in the age to come, eternal life (Mark 10:29–30).

The Lord asks for more than just accepting Him at the point of conversion. He asks if we'll follow Him every day. He wants permission to do new things in our lives, to heal and transform our thinking, feeling, and relating. As we surrender our personalities to Him, we receive the ability to serve God with peace and purpose. Jesus said, "Peace I leave with you, My peace I give to you; not as the world gives do I give to you. Let not your heart be troubled, neither let it be afraid" (John 14:27).

It is freeing to give up our fragmented natures and partial personality patterns. The dead ends these would lead to are replaced by the surprising adventures God has in store for us. God promises:

> Trust in the LORD with all your heart,
> And lean not on your own understanding;
> In all your ways acknowledge Him,
> And He shall direct your paths (Prov. 3:5–6).

Is it easy to draw upon the wisdom of God's psychology on a daily basis? No. Sometimes we feel frustrated and alone. Yet

Jesus promises, "I will never leave you nor forsake you" (Heb. 13:5). When I come to a crossroad in life and feel confused about which way to go, I ask God to open the right door and shut the others. Although I can feel exasperated waiting for the right door to open, I've noticed that when I walk through it His peace accompanies me.

Jesus was constantly surprising His disciples with innovative teachings and miracles of provision. He kept his followers on the edge of their seats. His resurrection on the heels of His death was the greatest surprise of all. Knowing that God is filled with surprises has helped me develop an adventurous spirit.

Still, I have to keep reminding myself that I'm not as capable of guiding my life as God is. Actually, I'm glad that I can't manipulate God into doing my will. Otherwise I would have missed the grand adventure.

DO YOU WANT
THE GRAND ADVENTURE?

The squiggly lines crisscrossed every which way, forming a latticework that looked like an abstract painting. I quickly sketched a replica for my lab notebook and removed the tissue sample from the electron microscope. *So that's what a human brain cell looks like. Far out!* Another student shuffled impatiently, waiting for his turn to gaze through the million-dollar lens.

I glanced at my watch as I walked down the hall of the six-story med school building to the student lounge. I had fifteen minutes for a cup of coffee; then I'd head down to the lab in the basement to get to know Howard better. Howard was the cadaver I'd been assigned for anatomy class.

I fairly glowed with pride this fifth week at the University of New Mexico School of Medicine, even though the studies were terribly hard. I'd been chosen as one of thirty-two students out of fifteen hundred applicants. My future looked bright.

I felt thankful to be in medical school. A full scholarship took care of board and tuition. Our family doctor had loaned me his old dissecting kit. Mom bought the textbooks I needed. My whole family was determined that I should do well. Since I had rededicated my life to Christ right before entering med school, I considered these provisions to be gifts from God.

The first day of classes, I admired the other students' brand-new lab coats. I was too broke to buy one, so I asked the Lord to help me out. The thought occurred to me to try a thrift store, even though it was a long shot. I drove over to one just as it was closing. I hurried in and plunged my arm halfway down into the first box I saw. My hand emerged, gripping a white lab coat exactly my size. Astonished, I exclaimed, "Thanks, God!" I paid the clerk fifty cents and dropped it off at a dry cleaner.

Now down in the anatomy lab, I lifted Howard the cadaver's left pectoral muscle and peeked underneath. I twanged a long yellow nerve with my probe. *Dan,* someone said. I glanced sideways before realizing that the voice came from within me. I stood transfixed, the probe in my right hand and scalpel in my left. *Dan, I never called you to be a physician,* whispered the still, small voice.

Is that You, God? I thought.

The message repeated: *I never called you to be a physician. If you want the grand adventure, you must follow Me.* Baffled by the clarity of the communication, I hurriedly scrubbed up and headed back to the lounge. I sat down in a daze.

The message felt authentic, yet it contradicted all of my career assumptions. *That voice couldn't have been God,* I reasoned. *He needs physicians in the world!* Hadn't God brought me here in the first place? But as I reflected further, I had to admit that I'd made my plans for medical school before I'd rededicated my life to Christ.

What is this grand adventure? I pondered. I didn't care to find out. Although I wasn't fond of science, a career as a physician was prestigious and lucrative. I shook off the message.

Our minds *need openness, discipline, and humility.* *Our* hearts *need friendship, trust, and intimacy.* Our bodies *need nutrition, sensitivity, and relaxation.* Our spirits *need salvation, renewal, and adventure.*

Over the next few weeks, I memorized the anatomy of the body and learned to spot subtle differences in tissue specimens. Although anatomy intrigued me, the other subjects didn't spark much interest. Biochemistry was murder. I passed my midterms, but not with flying colors. As the semester rushed to a close, I spent extra nights at the lab exploring the wonders of Howard.

One Friday night there was hardly a soul in the building. I got a cup of coffee and walked down the stairs and through the double doors. The freezing air made me shiver, but my fascination was piqued. Tonight, I was going to look inside Howard's heart.

I cut open the organ and felt surprised. The chambers of the heart were empty, now that Howard's blood no longer flowed through them. His heart—the seat of passion and meaning—was a void. A Scripture flashed through my mind:

All flesh is grass, . . .
The grass withers, the flower fades,
But the word of our God stands forever (Isa. 40:6–8).

I asked, "Howard, how did you live when you walked the earth—when your heart beat with life? Did you fall in love and get married? Did you have a good sex life? Did you become friends with your children? Did you know God?"

Suddenly, Howard's nerves, muscles, and tissues didn't matter to me anymore. A fire within me wanted to know what had motivated Howard, what had made him tick. Had he experienced a meaningful life? It struck me that those were not medical questions but questions of a psychological and spiritual nature.

That voice inside me—the voice that I'd pushed aside—spoke with gentle authority: *Dan, I never called you to be a physician. If you stay here, I will bless you, but you will miss the grand adventure. Will you follow Me?*

A chill shivered up my spine. *This must be God,* I thought.

I spoke out loud. "Okay, let's say it's really You talking to me,

God. What am I supposed to do—go to Idaho and dig potatoes? Don't you know that my family, my old professors, my new professors, and my family doctor will all reject me if I pick up and walk away?"

The voice repeated the question: *Will you follow Me?*

My stomach churned. My knees felt weak and unstable. I surveyed Howard and through him glimpsed all of humanity. Searing insights erupted out of my soul. *We all die,* I thought. *What matters is* how we live. *I don't want to be a plumber of the body; I want to be a healer of the soul.*

My scissors and scalpel clanked as I put them down on the metal tray. I looked at Howard through blurry eyes. I'd come to the lab to learn about aortas and ventricles. Howard's open heart taught me more than I'd bargained for.

Later that night as I lay in bed, I remembered how Gideon had received guidance in Old Testament times. He needed to determine whether or not God was guiding him into battle, so he placed some wool on the threshing floor and said, "If in the morning the fleece is wet and the ground is dry, I will know You are going to help me!" The next morning he wrung out a whole bowlful of water from the fleece.

I decided to place three fleeces before the Lord. "If this is really You talking to me," I said, "the answer is yes—I'll leave here and follow You. But I need a sign. Here are three things that are so impossible that I'll know it's You if they happen. First, I want the dean to say that I don't have to pay back the scholarship money. Second, I want the bookstore manager to give me a full refund for my books. Third, I'll need a job so that I don't starve while I'm waiting for the grand adventure." There was no answer—only the quiet glow of inner peace.

On Monday morning I made an appointment with the dean, whom I'd never met before. He was the final authority on all matters concerning students. My dread in facing him made it hard to breathe as I approached his office door. He greeted me with a hearty handshake. "What brings you here, Montgomery?" he asked. He waved for me to sit down in front of his massive oak desk.

My mouth felt dry as cotton. "Sir," I said, feeling heat redden my face, "God has told me to leave medical school."

The dean's smile changed into a look of horror and then disgust. "*Who* told you to leave?" he shouted, the color of his face matching his purple tie.

"God," I said, not wanting to elaborate.

I sat through a thirty-minute tirade, my hands and underarms sweating profusely. After he had spent his fury, he glared at me.

"I came here in good faith, and I have studied hard," I said. "But God is calling me out of medical school. Can you please arrange for me not to have to pay back my scholarship?"

He fumed and gagged as though he couldn't find words. Finally, his eyes narrowed, and he said in a razor sharp voice, "Montgomery, you're a discredit to this institution. Personally, I think you're a coward and a disgrace. But if you'll agree to see two psychiatrists tomorrow—and if they certify that you are sane—you can keep the scholarship money and leave!"

I left his office shaken, but aware that the first fleece had been answered. Next, I headed to the bookstore with an armload of textbooks. The clerk said flat out that they never gave full refunds. The manager overheard our conversation and asked why I was returning them.

"God has called me out of medical school," I said. "I need this money to live on."

He gave me two hundred dollars in cash.

The next morning and afternoon I endured two hour-long psychiatric interviews. I shared my story from beginning to end with each doctor. To my relief, they certified to the dean that I was sane.

One last fleece remained. I had gone to Sears that Saturday and filled out an application for employment. Thirty-one people were ahead of me on the hiring list. On Wednesday morning, I was munching snacks in the lounge, wondering if God was going to answer my fleece about a temporary job. My lab partner walked in.

"Hi, Dan," said Dee. He handed me a note. "Weird phone message from Sears. I figured it's a mistake. They said for you to report for work in the men's department tomorrow."

I snatched the note out of his hand. "Praise the Lord!" I yelled. He looked at me quizzically, for he had not known about my fleeces. "Dee," I said, "Jesus is alive and well. I just withdrew from school. I wish you the best. I've got to go."

I raced out through the glass front doors. An invisible cloud of glory encompassed me. A psalm came home to me with a force I'd never known:

Trust in the LORD, . . .
Delight yourself also in the LORD,
And He shall give you the desires of your heart (Ps. 37:3–4).

I left my friend Howard and the University of New Mexico School of Medicine that morning, leaping and praising God.

THE LORD IS TRUE
TO HIS WORD

For over twenty-five years now, I've passionately pursued my spiritual adventure. In turn, God has guided me to become a clinical psychologist, author, and speaker to thousands of people who want to transform their personalities in Christ.

I've experienced plenty of valleys on this road. But there is growth in the valley and joy on the occasional mountaintop.

Mostly, there is an abiding peace regardless of where I am on the road.

When you hear that still, small voice that no one else may understand or accept, remember that the Lord sees the beauty in the stone and may be cultivating your adventurous spirit.

Compass Counseling Overview

For a professional counselor or a curious layperson who may be interested in a deeper look at compass counseling, this appendix is a brief synopsis of compass theory.

Compass counseling is a Christian approach to brief counseling or long-term psychotherapy. Jesus Christ, the Son of God and Son of man, is the model for how a healthy personality functions. He is the standard against which human function and malfunction are gauged. The Holy Spirit, Christ's gift to every Christian, is the depth dimension of personality—a dynamic artesian well that flows through those who surrender to God, revealing the Father's love and will.

Compass counseling uses three major paradigms for describing and assessing personality: the spiritual core, the self compass, and the globe of human nature. These useful tools diagnose difficulties and promote growth toward health and wholeness.

THE SPIRITUAL CORE

The spiritual core—the center of being—is the source of our God-given personhood and Christ's presence within. Jesus said, "The kingdom of God is within you" (Luke 17:21). The Holy Spirit dwells within the core and inspires transformation in our personalities. The spiritual core is dynamic, not static, in nature. The core can be likened to an artesian well.

An artesian well is made by boring deep into the earth until water is reached, which then flows up by the force of internal pressure, like a fountain. The originating source of the water is always higher up, from the top of a hill or mountain.

From this high point, the water seeps down underneath the earth and converges into a mighty underground river. Because the well is drilled deep enough for its bottom to fall out, the core of the well connects to an endless supply of water. Effortlessly, the water from the underground river rises through the core of the well. An abundance of water is available at the surface of the artesian well. All that is required to keep the well flowing is for its core to stay clean and open.

Jesus said, "'He who believes in Me, as the Scripture has said, out of his heart will flow rivers of living water.' But this He spoke concerning the Spirit, whom those believing in Him would receive" (John 7:38–39).

One of the New Testament Greek words used for the Holy Spirit is *parakletos*. This translates as "One called alongside to help," "Comforter," or "Companion." These meanings clearly indicate the personal and intimate role of the Holy Spirit in the counseling process.

In coming home to the spiritual core, a person gives up a defensive style of living that is based on fear and manipulation, which theologically may be equated with sin. He or she adopts, instead, a growth-oriented lifestyle based on love, trust, and genuineness. God's love replaces fear as the motivating dynamic of life.

Because all human beings have felt the harsh impact of sin and evil, the core will reflect a mixture of fear and faith. Core pain results when we've been rejected, abandoned, or betrayed. Feelings of fear, pride, and defensiveness constrict the core.

Core trust, on the other hand, occurs in proportion to our experiences of love, trust, and grace. The inner ratio of fear versus faith is affected by how completely we surrender to the love and will of God and by how honestly we face our inner conflicts and work toward a healthy personality. A goal of compass counseling is to replace fear of life with faith in life.

THE SELF COMPASS

The self compass identifies the polarities of love and assertion, weakness and strength, as universal compass points of personality (LAWS). The theoretical underpinnings for this personality compass were derived from the collaborative work of Everett L. Shostrom and Dan Montgomery. (See *Handbook of Innovative Psychotherapies*[1] and *The Holy Spirit and Counseling*.[2])

This approach is not to oversimplify the complex nature of human beings. Many other qualities play an important role in shaping personality, such as masculinity and femininity, or extroversion and introversion. However, these four basic compass points of love and assertion, weakness and strength, provide clear latitude and longitude for assessing health in personality and relationships.

Partial Patterns in a Nutshell

In *How to Survive Practically Anything*, I define manipulation as "exploiting, using, and/or controlling another as a thing, rather than respecting and appreciating the other as a person."[3] Manipulative patterns originate as faulty ways of warding off anxiety and trying to control life. Manipulation works against the health of God's psychology by impairing personality wholeness and distorting relationships.

Gayle Erwin writes in *The Jesus Style,* "A particular characteristic of manipulation is that it destroys our ability to choose. It forces us to move defensively into the pattern or mold that others have chosen for us. Not a single person who tried to manipulate Jesus got the answer they expected. All of them received an expression of the true feelings of Jesus."[4]

Wilhelm Reich calls this defensive posturing *character armor;*[5] Eric Berne calls it a *negative life script;*[6] Carl Rogers calls it an *ideal self* versus the *real self;*[7] Aaron Beck calls it an *exaggerated process;*[8] Jacobi Moreno calls it the *loss of spontaneity and creativity;*[9] and Albert Ellis calls it a *set of irrational assumptions.*[10]

The eight partial personality patterns covered in this book employ distinctive manipulative strategies that a counselor must recognize and help to dismantle (see fig. A.1). Otherwise, the counselor is drawn into the manipulation and therapy is rendered ineffective.

Compass Counseling and DSM-IV

The self compass and the LAWS are practical tools that clarify the *Diagnostic and Statistical Manual of Mental Disorders,* or DSM-IV.[11] This manual is used worldwide and affords counselors a consensus for describing human behavioral dysfunction.

DSM-IV provides an especially effective classification for personality disorders. Mental health workers and pastoral counselors frequently encounter personality disorders in their counselees. By locating most of the personality disorders in DSM-IV on the self compass, compass counseling responds to a long-standing need for one central model that simultaneously accounts for health and dysfunction.

"The Compass Model" shows the dynamic range of human growth versus rigid stagnation (see fig. A.2). It is a diagnostic tool as well as a therapeutic tool. Through the discovery of exactly where and to what degree of severity a person is stuck, a counselor can generate a treatment plan.

God is a genius at guiding us to fulfill-ment within His over-all plans. He helps us find life's meaning in remarkable ways. The more we sur-render in love to God, the more He affirms our uniqueness and completes our destiny.

PARTIAL PATTERN	Manipulates Self by Being	Manipulates Others to Be
Dependent Clinging Vine	Needy; gullible; submissive; Pollyannish	Rescuing; supportive; strong; all-powerful
Histrionic Prima Donna	Hyperactive; giddy; flighty; petulant	Interested; admiring; doting; hyped
Paranoid Bully	Suspicious; attacking; oppositional; intimidating	Dependent; afraid; kowtowing
Antisocial Con Artist	Exploitive; conning; deceitful; abusive	Trusting; naive; vulnerable; easy marks
Avoidant Wallflower	Self-deprecating; expectant of rejection	Critical; demeaning; fed up; bored; rejecting
Schizoid Hermit	Self-sufficient loner; detached; indifferent	Frustrated; distant; helpless
Narcissistic Big Shot	Self-absorbed; demanding of special treatment	Subservient followers; hero worshipers
Compulsive Perfectionist	Rigid; self-righteous; managerial; indecisive	Obsequious; fawning; afraid to express themselves

FIGURE A.1

Views God as Being	Basic Belief System	Manipulative Strategy
A stern authority figure who commands obedience	"I always need help, support, and encouragement."	Seeks all-powerful partner; trusts authority figures
Intimate; fun; playful; spontaneous	"People exist to be excited about me. I am center stage."	Uses cuteness, tantrums, crying, dramatic gestures
Angry; fear-invoking; punishing	"Be wary. Hurt others before they hurt you. Don't yield."	Is defensive; interrogates and isolates those around him/her
Self-centered and able to use people to meet His own needs	"People are suckers; take what you need right now."	Charms; lies; steals; lives above the law
Distant; unforgiving; aloof; rejecting	"If people *really* knew me, they would reject me. I'm a misfit."	Hides from people; avoids opportunities for growth
Impersonal; unavailable; disinterested in human affairs	"Relationships are not worth it. People are irrelevant."	Stays away; is aloof; doesn't need or care for anyone
A fulfiller of one's hedonistic self-interest	"I'm better than others. I'm the flame; they are merely moths."	Mesmerizes others with own grandiosity
A compulsive rule maker and stern disciplinarian	"I uphold standards of perfection in all things."	Moralizes; lectures; finds fault and criticizes

PARTIAL PATTERNS IN A NUTSHELL

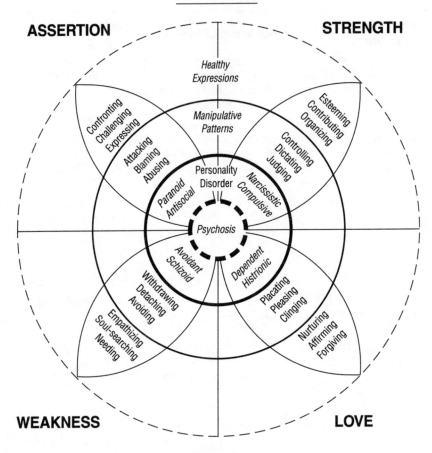

FIGURE A.2
THE COMPASS MODEL

The outermost level of "The Compass Model" is indicated by a semipermeable membrane that represents a discerning openness. When people are healthy, they express themselves directly without guile or manipulation. They experience and express love (nurturing, affirming, forgiving); assertion (expressing, challenging, confronting); weakness (empathizing, soul-searching, needing); and strength (organizing, contributing, esteeming). Their behavior is creative and trusting, like Christ's.

Compass counseling awakens and strengthens these wholesome personal and interpersonal behaviors.

The next level inward is called manipulative patterns. Here fear begins to overcome trust, resulting in people manipulating themselves and others.

To understand how fear works to constrict personality functioning, I use the analogy of the amoeba, a tiny one-cell animal. If an amoeba is repeatedly pricked by a pin, it permanently contracts itself to survive the attack. If a person is threatened psychologically or physically—especially early in life when basic personality is being formed—he or she learns to constrict awareness and thicken a defensive perimeter around the self.

Notice the slightly thicker ring surrounding the manipulative patterns. Fear shrinks behavioral options into defensive strategies. The love pole deteriorates into the manipulations of placating, pleasing, and clinging. The assertion pole rigidifies into abusing, blaming, and attacking. The weakness pole is distorted into withdrawing, detaching, and avoiding. The strength pole becomes judging, dictating, and controlling.

When people are stuck at the manipulative level of functioning, they may swing upward into more healthy expressions or downward into the next level of rigidity, called personality disorders.

The partial patterns or personality disorders described in this book are rigid ways of functioning, in which manipulation has become chronic and severe. Freedom, creativity, and spirituality are all but squeezed out of behavior, leaving only predictable partial patterns. Notice the even thicker ring of fear around the personality disorders.

Because the most common personality disorders are located on "The Compass Model," a counselor can immediately recognize what perpetuates a particular personality disorder and what growth stretches will lead to personality health. The dependent and histrionic disorders are located on the love pole. The antisocial and paranoid disorders are found on the assertion pole. The avoidant and schizoid disorders are located on the weakness pole.

People with narcissistic and compulsive disorders are stuck on the strength pole.

There remains one last level where the crisis of personality is so severe that the personality collapses into chaos. The most inward and contracted level of dysfunction is psychosis. The thick broken ring of this level shows the instability of psychosis.

The major psychoses can be predicted from "The Compass Model." People catastrophically stuck on the love pole deteriorate into psychotic depression and suicidal urges. People severely stuck on the assertion pole develop paranoid psychosis and become homicidal. Schizophrenia is the psychosis arising from extreme deterioration on the weakness pole. Manic striving is the psychotic symptomatology of the strength pole.

Compass counseling is a positive approach to healing the personality because "The Compass Model" demonstrates the bridge of continuity between psychopathology and personality health. Hope is ever present because rigidity is understood as a growth deficiency. The model shows what happens when growth is arrested and points the way to the growth stretches needed for health and wholeness.

Compass counseling

- educates counselees about what constitutes healthy personality and relationships.
- reveals partial personality patterns and self-defeating outcomes.
- assists people in taking responsibility for their lives.
- stimulates attitudinal and behavioral change by implementing growth stretches on repressed poles.
- brings about personality congruence as a counselee's thinking, feeling, sensing, and spiritual connection to God come into alignment.
- uses prayer to promote an intimate surrender to the guidance of the Holy Spirit from within the spiritual core.

Mixed Traits

"The Compass Model" helps pinpoint people's functioning even if they exhibit mixed traits. Mixed traits are unraveled by breaking them down into the component parts. For instance, a controlling person with dependent traits will have a predominant need for perfection and a secondary need for constant reassurance.

In this case a counselor works on growth stretches into the healthy dimensions of the weakness pole to balance out perfectionist control. Later, this can be followed by stretches into the assertion pole to balance out dependency. Gradually, the counselee loses the compulsion behind perfectionism and dependency and evolves a more whole personality.

THE GLOBE OF HUMAN NATURE

The globe of human nature integrates the four key elements of a human being into a whole nature (see fig. A.3). Instead of overemphasizing thinking, feeling, physiology, or spirituality, compass counseling says that the mind, heart, body, and spirit are *all* important.

God created all aspects of human nature and wants to see them flourish. Counselees need to become more aware of the various aspects of themselves that they may have ignored or repressed. Maturity means a well-developed self.

Compass theory asserts that Jesus Christ came to affirm our human natures as He did His own. He valued the sensations of His body, the feelings of His heart, the perceptions of His mind, and the guidance of the Holy Spirit. The Son of God and the Son of man lived wholeheartedly without being hindered by a partially functioning nature.

In the counseling process, God is invited to help counselees toward a recovery built upon all aspects of their natures.

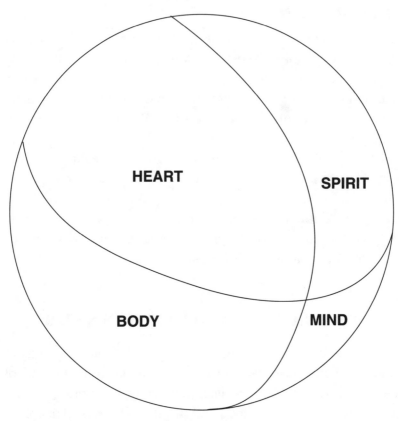

FIGURE A.3
GLOBE OF HUMAN NATURE

A counselor looks for the most underdeveloped or overly exaggerated aspect of a person's nature and then suggests growth stretches to help bring about a healthy human nature over time.

The aim is to mobilize the most blocked aspect of a person's nature. When there is an impasse in counseling, usually the person is overly relying on one aspect of his or her nature. A mind-oriented counselee blocks counseling by intellectualizing everything. A heart-oriented counselee throws up roadblocks by not engaging the mind. A body-oriented counselee is held captive to bodily appetites but lacks development in thinking, feeling, and prayer. A spirit-oriented counselee ignores emotions and bodily sensations.

The way through the counselee's particular impasse is to switch the therapeutic emphasis to the person's avoided aspects. For instance, a counselor would stimulate the feelings, sensations, and spirituality of the person who lives in the head. The counselor would stimulate the mind, heart, and body of the person who emphasizes only the spirit.

By shifting the therapeutic focus to the least-used aspects of the counselee's nature, growth stretches can be implemented that awaken and strengthen these dimensions.

Compass counseling uses the wisdom of God's psychology to develop well-functioning self compasses and enhance people's vital contact with their whole natures. A person may freely choose growth toward wholeness or resist that growth (see fig. A.4).

THE ROLE OF COMPASS COUNSELING

Compass counseling is not in competition with other approaches to counseling, whether contemporary or traditional. The principles of compass counseling are available to serve the practitioners of any system that assists people in growth and change. These principles are also applicable in education, church life, marriage enrichment, child rearing, and psychiatry.

Resistance to Growth
RIGIDITY Doing the same thing again and again with no new learning. Beating our heads against a brick wall instead of looking for the corner. Being stuck in a rut. Having a partial personality that overrides the potential for awareness, choice, and growth.
DEADNESS Being inflexible and fixed in our framework of living. Being repressed and defensive. Living on automatic pilot. Plodding through life mechanically. Having tunnel vision. Hiding our hearts. Having a frozen self compass. Controlling others or being controlled by them.
DISTORTIONS OF LOVE Manipulating ourselves and others through the roles of clinging vine, prima donna, bully, con artist, wallflower, hermit, big shot, and perfectionist. Using every means to get love other than being our real selves. Not facing ourselves or relating intimately with others.
STAGNATION Being mounted like a dead butterfly instead of soaring like a live one. Being in a state of psycho-spiritual rigor mortis. Being driven by fear, resentment, and defensiveness. Living in self-will with false pride. Neglecting our inner calling from Christ. Wasting our God-given potential. Missing the adventure of living.

FIGURE A.4

God's Psychology

GROWING IN GRACE

Responding to the Word of God and the Holy Spirit. Discovering novel solutions to new problems and creative solutions to old problems. Having a childlike trust in God and openness to the whole personality. Displaying a willingness to grow and learn through life.

ALIVENESS

Having a humble mind, an intimate heart, a vital body, and an adventurous spirit. Being aware of and expressive of love, assertion, weakness, and strength. Learning from everything that happens. Using God's psychology to live honestly and wholeheartedly.

HEALTHY LOVE

Expressing ourselves sincerely and diplomatically. Having empathy for others' hurts, hopes, and needs. Being patient with our weaknesses and those of others. Forgiving wrongs and making amends. Using the self compass as a tool for loving ourselves, loving others, and loving God.

TRANSFORMATION

Experiencing the many miracles of life. Being intimate with God and seeking our heart's desires. Being of good cheer. Being healers, forgivers, and givers of faith in God. Accepting imperfections while growing toward wholeness. Asking the Holy Spirit for daily comfort and guidance. Seeing beauty in the stone.

FIGURE A.4 (CONTINUED)

Individual
Study Guide

This study guide is designed to stimulate your adventures in the sometimes difficult, sometimes wonderful, process of self-discovery. May the wisdom of God's psychology assist you in the process of finding beauty in the stone.

PART 1: THE SELF COMPASS

Chapter 1: Are There Laws of Personality?

1. Jesus is called the Rose of Sharon, the Lion of Judah, the Lamb of God, and the Prince of Peace. Put these four names at the top of a sheet of paper and go down each column, briefly describing ways that you have experienced being a rose, a lion, a lamb, and a peacemaker. If one column is especially short, take active growth stretches in that direction.

Pray for the Holy Spirit to reveal to you more of the health in Jesus' personality.

2. This week explain the self compass to someone. Can you explore together how the compass might help him or her?

3. In your journal or on a sheet of paper, explain how we can be unique individuals in Christ, even though the self compass is universal.

Chapter 2: Roughly Hewed Stones

1. I share about the shock I first felt when I learned in my psychology training that I wasn't as perfect as I thought. At what points in this book have you felt the shock of imperfection? Can you go back to these sections and prayerfully read them a second time?

2. In your next season of prayer, picture yourself as a roughly hewed stone in the Master's hands. How are you willing to allow Him to do some polishing on you? Can you surrender specific rough spots, asking for His help?

PART 2: PARTIAL PERSONALITY PATTERNS

Chapters 3 through 10: Clinging Vines; Prima Donnas; Bullies; Con Artists; Wallflowers; Hermits; Big Shots; Perfectionists

Please see the growth stretches listed at the end of each of these chapters. They provide suggestions pertinent to each specific rigidity.

PART 3: VIRTUES OF GOD'S PSYCHOLOGY

Chapter 11: Purifying Your Personality

1. Isn't it a relief to know that within each rigid pattern, there is a gem of great price—a virtue? Once you are set loose from your rigidities, many creative options are available to you. Virtues that eluded you for years appear with relative ease.

Put a square around the virtues that you need to add to your personality. Circle the virtues that already abide within you. Look for these virtues in others, and compliment others when you find them:

Charity	Good cheer	Courage	Creativity
Empathy	Objectivity	Discipline	Autonomy

2. Do you agree that churches can have a group personality? How would you describe the church you're now in? How would you characterize the church in which you grew up? If your present church could be healthier, can you think of ways to help it become so? Would a book study of *Beauty in the Stone* in an adult class or prayer group provide people with some tools for transformation?

Chapter 12: Change in Your Own Backyard

1. What is your reaction to this story about Danny Charles and his mother? What makes it possible for people to change, even in fundamental ways, until they die?

2. Form a prayerful vision of change for a family member with whom you've had conflict. Ask God to help you and this person find the pathway to intimacy, even though it may seem impossible. This week take any steps that come to you for moving toward honest leveling and the hope of reconciliation.

PART 4: GLOBE OF HUMAN NATURE

Chapter 13: Your Human Nature

1. Draw a globe of human nature, representing how your mind, heart, body, and spirit balance out. If you think one aspect dominates, make this part of your globe larger than the rest. If one or more are rarely used, make them smaller. Use pens of various colors to fill in each aspect of your nature with a color that symbolizes that aspect to you.

2. Pray for the Holy Spirit to expand your awareness for the full use of your nature so that in the future, all aspects come to be equal in size and unique to you.

Chapter 14: A Humble Mind

1. Where are you between discipline and spontaneity? If you are stuck on one side or the other, practice skating to the opposite side more often. If you're too disciplined, deliberately set aside time for play, recreation, and frivolity. If you're too spontaneous, put new energy into planning, organization, and follow-through.

Chapter 15: An Intimate Heart

1. Write in a journal about which of the following stages of intimacy you have the most trouble with.

- Mutual trust
- How to "take the elevator down"
- The rhythm of restraint and expression
- How to modulate feelings

Talk over your fears or reservations with a friend. Explore events from the past that may be making you gun-shy about feeling close to others. If your feelings are too painful, consider professional counseling.

2. In your Bible reading, mark verses that encourage each of these steps and memorize them.

3. Think about how Jesus found intimacy of the heart with His inner circle of confidants. Ask Him to help you do the same.

Chapter 16: A Vital Body

1. If you suffer from depression, make an appointment with a psychologist or pastoral counselor to talk it over. Find out if you need help in grieving a loss, if you need fresh spiritual direction, or if you have a biochemical disorder requiring an antidepressant.

2. Become aware if you have a bias against your body. This could arise from early childhood training or from viewing the body as corrupt or ungodly. Are you willing to revise these perceptions? Jesus enjoyed His body and wasn't afraid to feel pleasure in His senses. Can you develop a more sensorial spirituality by enjoying the world that God has given us? Try savoring the food you taste, listening to the sounds of nature, and hugging friends and family.

3. Ponder and pray about any additional steps to help your body be more vital. What about treating your body to

- Fresh fruits and vegetables
- A quiet walk
- Long soaks in the tub
- Fitness center workouts
- Water aerobics
- Swimming or bicycling

Chapter 17: An Adventurous Spirit

1. Keep a prayer journal. Buy one that appeals to you, and keep it by your bed. Write in it before you go to sleep, after you've prayed. Note the different prayers you say to God and the responses you get. Be real with Him.

Remember to record anything that happens during the day that seems to be spiritually guided. Underline things that are especially meaningful. After a month or so, reread your journal. Identify major themes of your life and see how God is guiding you. What is your grand adventure?

Group
Book Study

Dear Leader,

Here are twelve suggestions for starting a *Beauty in the Stone* book study in your adult church class, neighborhood, or home prayer meeting.

1. Ask your local Christian bookstore manager to stock books for interested friends, acquaintances, and church members.

2. Tell people that you are interested in facilitating a group that will begin as soon as you have three or more members. List names and phone numbers of interested persons. If you are already in an existing class or prayer group, suggest that the focus might be on a book study process for several months.

3. Set a starting date and overall time frame. I suggest one hour per week for about twenty-five weeks, or until the book is completed.

4. Start each meeting with at least five minutes of prayer time. Let people pray silently or out loud for the presence of God to guide the group's progress.

5. The book study is carried on in a round-robin fashion. Each person reads three or so paragraphs, then shares experiences, needs, and hopes. As the group leader, you are but a trusted

servant, not a dictator or monopolizer. Let people share (you may need to set an agreed-upon time limit of three to five minutes). Then invite the next reader to begin. If a person reads and wishes not to express a personal comment, he or she is free to do so.

6. Explain to members that there is no cross talk, judgment, or advice giving. Individuals are free to express personal experiences but must withhold comments about others. Stress the need for confidentiality, which is the lifeblood of self-disclosure and trust.

7. Trust the group process and the presence of the Holy Spirit to draw people out and help them to be healed. Develop a warm interpersonal climate free from moralizing.

8. Anything human is worthy of understanding. Christ accepts us as we are and desires us to become more real. People are healed and encouraged when they confide from the heart: "Confess your trespasses to one another, and pray for one another, that you may be healed" (James 5:16). If a member tells another member what to do or not do, jump in with a gentle reminder that there should be no cross talk, judgment, or advice giving.

9. With ten minutes remaining, announce that only one or two more people can read or share. With five minutes left, ask everyone to mark the stopping point in the book. Stand up. Join hands. Invite someone to lead the Lord's Prayer.

10. Dismiss the group on time. Allow people to mill around.

11. When the book study has been completed, take a vote to see whether the group wishes to begin a new cycle at the beginning of the book. If so, let a new volunteer take over the servant/leader role. Pass these guidelines to the new volunteer.

12. A *Beauty in the Stone* book study can be open-ended and run year-round. Newcomers can join the group at any time and continue as long as they wish. The only criterion for membership is the desire to experience God at work within your personality.

God bless you and stay in touch,
Dan Montgomery, Ph.D.

Notes

Chapter 3

1. Frederick S. Perls, *Gestalt Therapy Verbatim* (Moab, Utah: Real People Press, 1969), p. 33.

Chapter 7

1. *The Journals of Kierkegaard,* ed. Alexander Dru (New York: Harper and Row, 1959), p. 243.

2. Theodore Millon, *Disorders of Personality* (New York: John Wiley & Sons, 1981), p. 61.

3. Paul Tournier, *The Strong and the Weak* (Philadelphia: Westminster, 1963), p. 27.

Chapter 8

1. Rollo May, *Man's Search for Himself* (New York: Norton, 1953), p. 34.

Chapter 9

1. Harold C. Schonberg, *Lives of the Great Composers* (New York: Norton, 1970), p. 265.

Chapter 10

1. Adrian van Kaam, *Religion and Personality* (Englewood Cliffs, N.J.: Prentice-Hall, 1964), p. 158.

Chapter 11

1. Charles Stanley, *The Wonderful Spirit-Filled Life* (Nashville: Thomas Nelson, 1992), p. 145.

Chapter 14

1. Gabriel Marcel, *Creative Fidelity* (New York: Farrar and Straus, 1964).

2. Henri Nouwen, *Reaching Out: The Three Movements of the Spiritual Life* (New York: Doubleday, 1975), p. 12.

3. Eugene Peterson, *The Message* (Colorado Springs: NavPress, 1993), p. 20.

Chapter 15

1. Sidney Jourard, *The Transparent Self,* 2d ed. (New York: Van Nostrand, 1971).

Chapter 16

1. Howard Bartley, *Principles of Perception* (New York: Harper and Row, 1958), p. 459.

2. Grace Stuart, *Narcissus: A Psychological Study of Self-Love* (New York: Macmillan, 1955).

Appendix

1. Raymond Corsini, ed., *Handbook of Innovative Psychotherapies* (New York: John Wiley & Sons, 1982), chapter one.

2. Marvin G. Gilbert and Raymond T. Brock, eds., *The Holy Spirit and Counseling, Vol. I: Theology and Theory* (Peabody, Mass.: Hendrickson, 1985), chapter sixteen.

3. Dan Montgomery, *How to Survive Practically Anything* (Ann Arbor, Mich.: Servant Publications, 1993).

4. Gayle D. Erwin, *The Jesus Style* (Waco: Word, 1988).

5. Wilhelm Reich, *Character Analysis* (New York: Pocket Books, 1976).

6. Eric Berne, *Games People Play* (New York: Ballantine, 1985).

7. Carl Rogers, *On Becoming a Person* (Boston: Houghton Mifflin, 1995).

8. Aaron Beck and Arthur Freeman, *Cognitive Therapy of Personality Disorders* (New York: The Guilford Press, 1990).

9. Jacobi Moreno, *Psychodrama, Vol. 1,* fourth ed. (Beacon, New York: Beacon House, 1972).

10. Albert Ellis, *Reason and Emotion in Psychotherapy* (New York: Carol Publishing Group, 1994).

11. American Psychiatric Association, *Diagnostic and Statistical Manual of Mental Disorders,* fourth ed. (Washington, D.C.: American Psychiatric Association, 1994).